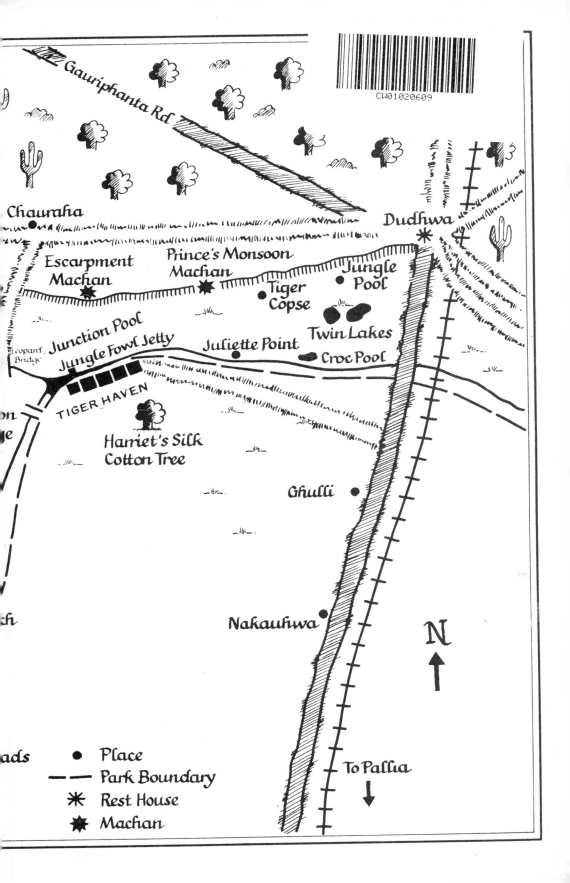

The
LEGEND
of the
MANEATER

By the same author

Tiger Haven
Tara, a Tigress
Prince of Cats
Tiger! Tiger
Eeelie and the Big Cats

The
LEGEND
of the
MANEATER

by

ARJAN SINGH

RAVI DAYAL Publisher
Delhi

Published by

RAVI DAYAL Publisher
51 E Sujan Singh Park
New Delhi 110003

Distributed by

ORIENT LONGMAN LTD
Bangalore Bombay Calcutta
Guwahati Hyderabad Madras Lucknow
New Delhi Patna

ISBN 0 86311 450 4

Typeset by Resodyn, New Delhi 110030
Printed at Rekha Printers Pvt. Ltd., New Delhi 110020

for
John Aspinall

Acknowledgements

MY gratitude to John Aspinall for writing a Foreword to this book, and for his material and moral support over the years is unbounded. By ascribing a dignity to mammals he has confirmed the pinchbeck and condescending attitude of the human towards other life forms. The bars of his zoos at Howletts and Port Lympne are confines only to the physical, and not the spirit, of the wild. The empathy of those concerned with the welfare of higher mammals and their responses are examples which could well be followed by wilderness conservators, and zoo keepers alike.

By the posthumous examples of my father and elder brother, I have paid tributes to qualities of achievement which go to the making of complete human beings, and which by precept have influenced my attitudes. By reference to a byegone age of more gracious existence, and forbearance, I have emphasized the competitive motivations of an overcrowded planet, and a future of despair.

I am greatly indebted to my sister-in-law, Mira, who once again typed the manuscript, to my niece Brinda who found me a publisher, to my sister Amar, and cousin Mahindar Singh, who have put certain family connections in perspective; to Minu Ismail who has made various suggestions regarding the days in Balrampur; to Geoff and Diane Ward of the USA who have reacted favourably to the script, and who suggested an autobiographical slant, to demonstrate the circumstances leading to a concern for the Maneater; I was initially unwilling to comply with this suggestion since there is so much suffering humanity to look to; to Duff Hart-Davies of the UK, my valued colleague, and a hunter, who encouraged me to overcome my unwillingness to start writing, and my doubts as to where to begin, by suggesting that I should start at page 1, go on to 2 and 3 and so on! And he has since expressed his great enthusiasm over the rough hewn typescript.

And to Tara, who has disappeared from the Tiger Haven Range in her sixteenth year, her confreres, and her progeny who still stalk the forests of the night, I bow my head in homage to a noble predator, for to my mind, like old soldiers, they never die—they only fade away.

Foreword

THIS book, probably the last that Arjan Singh will ever write, is a *cri de coeur*. Indeed, it is from the heart that he has always written and now, as these pages pass before you, you can look into the agony of his own soul. Everything that he has feared has come to pass and the wild creatures that he spent the latter half of his life protecting are slipping away before our eyes.

Recent press reports tell us that tiger numbers have shrunk dramatically over the last ten years. India's wildlife reserves support just over a thousand animals. The overflow of tigers into unprotected forests is estimated at 2,500. The numbers have halved in the last twenty years. Three of the eight subspecies have been recently wiped out, the Persian, Balinese and Javan. The great Siberian race now numbers less than two hundred in the wild. On the Chinese side of their range, fifty have been killed in the last two years—for medicinal purposes. The South China tiger now numbers less than eighty, while the Sumatran tiger is down to a few hundred. It would appear that the whole species is in terminal decline. As the tiger is a classic example of a flagship, or, as Arjan Singh prefers, an 'indicator' species, this is very bad news for the remaining pockets of wildlife. This book is an important one as it lays bare the predicament of wild nature today. The author is one of few who saw the portents long ago and acted on them. I remember him telling me when I was in Tiger Haven twenty years ago that the statistics as to tiger populations put about by the Indian Forestry and Wildlife Departments were fabricated and massaged upwards to please the international wildlife organizations that fed them money. Arjan Singh also told me that forestry officials reported back to the government figures that bore scant relation to the truth. Even today India is supposed to have officially 11 per cent forest cover. The reality is that between 2 and 3 per cent of canopy forest remains.

Though Arjan Singh was befriended by Indira Gandhi and been

recognized throughout the world for his field work, being awarded the World Wildlife Fund Gold Medal in 1976, he is of a temperament that has little empathy for bureaucrats and place men. He likes best to work at Tiger Haven in the company of tigers, leopards and fishing cats with whom in turn he has developed the most extraordinary relationships. As a halfway house between man and wilderness, Tiger Haven could be compared to Kora on the Tana river in Kenya where George Adamson spent the last decade of his life. Adamson and Singh are unusual in that they crossed an emotional threshold and physically embraced the animals they protected. Both forged bonds with some of the creatures in their care. Let us all hope that Tiger Haven does not meet the fate of Kora—abandoned and forgotten within a few months of its founder's heroic death at the hands of poachers.

A scion of a princely house, Arjan Singh is a reformed hunter. The great work that he has done and the example he has set has fully expiated his early transgressions. Who else has put a tiger and an Indian leopard born in zoos back to the wild and then seen them breed? A remarkable pioneering achievement. Like all men who break new ground, he has drawn his share of criticism—particularly of course from the experts. In this context, envy is the tribute that mediocrity constantly pays to genius.

John Aspinall

Contents

Plates

(following page 96)

Introduction

BY propagating the Cult of the Maneater human beings have expressed their abhorrence of, and attributed an ultimate depravity to, the tiger for not obeying man-made laws. In this, my last book on the subject, I have endeavoured with the limited eloquence at my command to dispute an entire gamut of clichés which have accumulated over the ages and seem likely to provide the epitaph for the passing of the great predators. Many million years of evolution will then disappear into limbo before the untrammelled growth and unrestrained demands of the human race.

As this magnificent cat prepares to enter the portals of Valhalla I have tried to clear its name of the infamy which has been heaped upon it, and which provides the *raison d'etre* for its slaughter. But it is now probably too late to ensure a future. The tiger was once destroyed by humans as a competitor: his sheer magnificence, his power, his beauty, the mystery of his life, became targets for destruction to inflate human egos. Yet the tiger still had a chance, for human aspirations which can, on occasions, aspire to godhead, could not permit the values embodied by the tiger to pass from the planet. But now the end is of necessity more insidious and clinical, and the tiger must go because there is no room for him in a shrinking world where might is right, with the human both judge and jury, and always supposedly in the right.

The solitary predator has a nobility of character within his natural limitations. The tiger or leopard will take prey to their offspring and allow them to feed first. They will sit around, and await their turn at kills, subject to the priority of the killer, and adults seldom feed at the same time. Glowing eyes in flashlight photographs provide proof of their patience. Their unblemished countenances are a tribute to a well established feeding protocol.

With the social predator the struggle for existence intensifies. The lioness will hunt for the pride, but the lion appropriates the kill. He will swat the cubs out of the way if there is not enough to go round. Lions will crowd a kill, fighting and squabbling for the major share, their scarred visages a hallmark of social competitive living and almost a reflexion of the wounded human psyche. Thus the growth of social and competitive living has suppressed individual characteristics, and each succeeding generation brings to the fore its own traumas.

The human in intraspecific competition must function within certain legal limits, but for other animals there is no supporting justice, and, in fact, sport hunting justifies an eventual genocide. Many ungulates confirm their existence by measuring up to their usage by man, but for the predator there is no reprieve. The major predators live in 'Third World' countries, and must vanish in the face of an uncontrollable population increase. But this facet has only been highlighted by the emergence of international wildlife forums initiated by 'developed' countries. Nevertheless, these developed countries, who are so keen on preserving the great predators, have none of their own. 'Save the tiger, but save him in your own country' they say. The predators are unwelcome in the countries of their origin, whether they be in Australia or Alaska. Wolves have been extirpated in Europe; and the Lynx, reintroduced into Switzerland, the citadel of conservation, faces a doubtful future. The hunter lobby lays claim to the essential culling of ungulates in relation to the bio-mass, but in fact it dishonestly juggles the available land mass figures to create a surplus of animals, thus justifying hunting, the slaughter of prime breeders, and the debasement of herds. In contrast, the predator keeps animal populations young and free of debasement, for they prey only on stragglers and the incapacitated.

But the bell has now tolled, and the portents are everywhere. The famous zoos of London and Whipsnade are up for sale. Safari Parks are reducing the feed of their predator populations as their profits fall, until like Lion Country Safari in the Laguna Hills of California, they shut down for good. Zoos have extended their claims of usefulness from being mere centres of entertainment to that of breeding endangered species for reintroduction into the wilds; but these claims are entirely illusory. No zoo is directly affiliated with the restocking of any wilderness area, and the result is an ad hoc breeding, meticulous and meaningless maintenance of subspecies' stud books, limited exchange between zoos, and an obligatory euthanasia of surplus populations as the bottom falls out of the market. Traditional zoos with their alleged utilities are in reality animal prisons:

All England's fame: condensed in name: You'll find in fat
'Who's Who':
But all her shame: Through hunt and game: Is writ in sad
'Whose Zoo';

Whose Zoo is it: Where proud lions sit: and yawn their lives
away:
While through the bars: They sense the stars: Where unbound
kingdoms lay?

Whose Zoo is it: Where eagles flit: Their winged thoughts all
but clipped:
And Man stands there: To gape and stare: Of all compassion
stripped?

Hyman Segal

But what has the future in store for these masterpieces of evolution? Why are zoos closing down? Have they lost their appeal, and can their income no longer match their expenditure? When the San Diego zoo and the Bronx in New York, and their Endangered Species programmes are no more, and wilderness areas in 'Third World' countries are crowded into fragmented pockets by surging populations, that will be the end; for then there will be no room for wild animals.

The only hope is for wildlife to become an international subject; each 'Third World' country desirous of preserving its wildlife should seek an affiliation with developed countries and their zoos. And wilderness areas must be excluded from human usage.

I suggest a readjustment of the attitudes of human beings towards animals. Progress is measured by a successful adaptation to changing circumstances, and if we are to preserve the animal world against the onslaught of various forms of human administration, medieval policies must now change to the preservation of a microcosm. By reading the case histories in the book of a dozen so-called maneaters, let us understand that they became maneaters because human beings forced them to become so.

This book is written with a definite purpose—it aims to spread the message that wildlife, and in particular the tiger and other predators, must be protected far more effectively than at present. This is essential not only because animals are wonderful in themselves, but because their presence in the wild is the surest way of stemming environmental degradation and the best indicator of the environmental health of our planet. In order to strengthen my central argument, I have freely used material from two of my previous books, *Tiger Haven* (1973) and *Tiger! Tiger* (1984), both now out of print. Readers of these two books will no doubt recognize some of the tigers, characters and situations featuring in the succeeding chapters. I make no apologies for such recapitulation if it contributes towards fulfilling the purpose of this my final book and, indeed, of my life.

1 Early Days

I was born in Gorakhpur in the United Provinces (now called Uttar Pradesh) on 15 August 1917. My father was posted there as a Deputy Collector. The administration of India was dominated by members of the Indian Civil Service or I.C.S., who were mostly recruited through a competitive examination, held in England, and naturally consisted largely of Englishmen, though a limited recruitment of Indians was also allowed. The lower echelon of administrators was manned by the Provincial Civil Service and was locally recruited by examination or by nomination. My father was nominated to a special cadre of the P.C.S., and he was posted during the course of his tenure to Gorakhpur, one of the eastern districts of U.P.

Jasbir, my father, was the youngest of nine children of Raja Sir Harnam Singh. A brother, Inderjit Singh, was killed in World War I while serving as a captain in the Medical Corps where he was awarded the MC, while two other brothers died at birth. My paternal grandfather, Harnam Singh, was the younger son of Randhir Singh, the Maharaja of Kapurthala. The rulers of the State had sided with Maharaja Ranjit Singh in the Sikh Wars, but during the Mutiny of 1857 Randhir Singh marched into Oudh with his troops in support of the British. For this act of loyalty he was ceded Grants in the districts of Kheri and Bahraich in U.P. and, as a result, became one of the biggest taluqdars in the State; his lands here yielded a greater revenue than those in the Punjab. Randhir became a favourite at the Court of Queen Victoria and married an English woman who was addressed as Lady Randhir Singh. Though she was not officially recognized as the Maharani, he was greatly under her influence, and, indeed, at one time considered embracing Christianity. Interestingly enough, in 1860 Randhir Singh Ahluwalia was one of the witnesses at the wedding of my mother's grandparents, Captain Dupre Payne, then on a posting with the State Forces of Kapurthala, and Mary Alicia Williamson.

Maharaja Randhir Singh had two sons, of whom the elder, Kharak

Singh, succeeded to the Kapurthala throne. He died without any issue, and normally my grandfather should have become the Maharaja. However, thanks to the machinations of antagonistic courtiers, a bribed British Resident, and a pliable Civil Surgeon who declared the Maharani to be pregnant when her husband was on his death bed, an unrelated child was smuggled into the palace and became heir to the Kapurthala throne. Harnam Singh made numerous representations to the Government of India and the Privy Council, but despite the admission of the Maharani (who sent for my grandfather when she was dying, and admitted that she had sinned against his interests), the Empire stood firm. It did not wish to reverse a decision and expose the corrupt practices of British administrators. Thus, the adopted son, Jagatjit Singh, was permitted to remain the ruler. But in an effort to make amends, grandfather was made a hereditary Raja, awarded a knighthood and a KCSI, and given the administration of the Oudh properties for his lifetime: an action objected to by Jagatjit Singh, but this time without avail.

Grandfather was banished to live on the Oudh properties and in Jullundur, where he came under the influence of the Reverend Golaknath. Perhaps as a reaction to the unjust usurpation of his inheritance, the predilection of his father for the Christian faith, and the persuasive proselytization of Golakhnath, whose relative Priscilla he married, Grandfather changed his faith and forfeited forever his chances of acquiring the Kapurthala Gaddi—it was the policy of the British not to allow a change of religion among Ruling Princes. However, a handsome income enabled him to augment his wealth, which he enhanced further by lending money to impecunious landlords. A later story relates that he wanted to revert to Sikhism, but Golaknath guarded his prestigious convert with great devotion, even to the extent of sleeping across the door of grandfather's bedroom at night.

Grandfather had a remarkable physical presence, and it was said that at the time of his death at over eighty he had lost only one tooth, broken when falling over a tent rope many years earlier! Besides being very strong, he had the largest and most hypnotic eyes I recall seeing on a human being, which, combined with a slightly bloodshot appearance (caused, perhaps by the large pegs of Scotch that he imbibed every evening) gave him an awe-inspiring personality. He also had a flaring temper and, according to Sir Penderel Moon, a distinguished British administrator, that was one of the reasons why he was side-tracked for the throne of Kapurthala. My brother and I were his favourites, and he insisted on our sitting by him endlessly in the evenings when he had his whisky as he indulged in an elaborate dressing session. We nevertheless stood in awe of him. Once, when we were spending a week-end with him at The Manor, his family mansion in Simla, he discovered that we had been teasing one of his visitors—whereupon he advanced on us where we were sitting in the summerhouse; Jumper, my brother, saw him first and ran traitorously into the garden, while I had my back to his approach and sat in petrified silence until a heavy slap bestirred me, and I followed my brother at speed.

My father was born in 1889. He first went to college at Forman Christian College in Lahore, and subsequently he was sent to Balliol College, Oxford—a somewhat unfortunate choice, for Balliol is a scholars' college, and my father, though a fine sportsman, could not lay claim to any great aptitude for studies.

Mother, christened Mabel, was born in 1888 to Edward Golaknath, a relative of my grandmother, stationed at Jullundur as a Deputy Inspector of Police, and Eleanor Payne, the daughter of Dupre Payne, a captain in the 7th Fusiliers. However, she was brought up by the Reverend William Golakhnath in Jullundur, and subsequently sent to the University of Indiana in Indianapolis to study and be trained as a kindergarten teacher. Unlike Father, who was always boasting of his aristocratic lineage, Mother never spoke to me of her parents, though she had a great love for William Golaknath and his wife. She does not appear to have taught for any length of time, and was married to my father on New Year's Eve, 1914.

Jaswant, nicknamed Jumper because of his inability to pronounce his own name, was the eldest son, and born in 1915 at Budaon. I followed two years later at Gorakhpur. My earliest recollection is of our arrival at Balrampur late at night in 1923. I don't know why this event sticks in my mind, because the subsequent process of settling in is a blank, and my next vivid recollections are those of my associates once we had become residents, but without firm dates.

Feudal principalities in India under the British consisted of Ruling Chiefs who functioned with the honorific title of His Highness and were virtually independent for purposes of internal administration, subject to general supervision by the States Department of the Central Government. They had various privileges, and were entitled to a salute of a number of guns according to the size of the State. For instance, the Nizam of Hyderabad had a 21- gun salute, and the lowest in the rank of precedence had eight guns.

In U.P., a second rank of Chieftains were the taluqdars. They were not Ruling Chiefs, had fewer privileges, and had among their ranks some landlords who were masters of only a single village. They owed allegiance to the Court of Wards, a provincial administrative organization which supervised the functioning of the feudal chieftains or taluqdars. Of these, the largest and the richest was Balrampur, which in my early years had an income of almost half a million rupees. A provision in the Court of Wards functioning procedure specified that, should a taluqdar happen to be a minor, or if the estate was badly administered, the Provincial administration could assume its governance until such time as conditions became suitable for the local ruler to resume administration. It was when the Maharaja of Balrampur was a minor, and also not completely *compos mentis*, that my father was posted to the Court of Wards as Special Manager, Balrampur Estate, by the provincial government.

My earliest recollection of childhood companions is of a boy called Minu Ismail, the youngest in a family of three sons and a daughter of Lillian and Professor Ismail of Forman Christian College, Lahore. Belonging to a family of six brothers in a Christian family surnamed Gilani, from the tehsil of Jagraon, Lillian, a well known beauty of Lahore, had made her home with Percy, whom we knew as Gilan, one of her brothers. He was Agricultural Adviser to the Maharaja of Balrampur.

Minu was two years older than I and, as he remained in Balrampur when his brothers and sister were educated elsewhere, I saw much more of him than of the other two. Parvez, the eldest, was quite a bit older than us, and as an occasional visitor we looked upon him as a hero. He was extremely keen on wrestling and physical exercise, and had a magnificent physique. He had a very fine singing voice, and was academically brilliant; he entered the Indian Civil Service with high marks. His younger brother, Peroz, also had a good physique, was an excellent artist, but was too much of a scamp to take life seriously. He had a very keen eye for the girls and, being closer to our age, we looked forward to his visits. He was not only our leader, but also a most entertaining companion. Zuhra, the sister, did not come much into our ken when she came on holiday from Dehra Dun where she was studying, and the only excitement she created was when she had an unfortunate affair and married a boy belonging to the local clan of Bhayas, who happened to be a Ward of my father.

It is difficult to remember after so many years when Minu and I established a rapport, and, though we were of the same age group, my recollections are of an excellent raconteur who brought my brother and me news of the Dempsey–Tunney fight on 23 September 1926. This was followed a year later by the 'Battle of the Long Count' in which Tunney retained the title of World Heavyweight Boxing Champion. Minu also entertained us with stories of Tarzan, though I am unable to recall whether he had acquired his knowledge from the Tarzan books, which were the current rage, or whether from films, which we avidly looked forward to seeing after Minu's dramatic rendition of the adventures of the erstwhile Lord Greystoke and Jane Porter. I have vivid recollections of the great head of the MGM lion and of the magnificent physique of Elmo Lincoln, the then Tarzan. The films were, of course, silent and in black and white, with written captions explaining the sequence of events. We watched the yellow tinged pictures with fascination as all the characters introduced by Minu came alive on the screen. Tantor the elephant, Numa the lion, Sabor the lioness, the Tarmangani, the Gomangani, and Korak the King Ape. Minu's repertoire also included the adventures of Tom Mix, of Rin Tin Tin, Rudolf Valentino in the *Son of the Sheik*, and Douglas Fairbanks in *Thief of Baghdad*. We followed the Pickfair affair, the romance of Douglas Fairbanks Sr and Mary Pickford, with great interest.

But all of Minu's tales were not garnered from films, and his fertile imagination would entertain us with tales of how he was chased by wolves when riding his Rudge Whitworth racing cycle, and how he dramatically dismounted and tore the wolf's jaws asunder. Not to be outdone, I recall that I riposted by describing an incident where I was charged by a large king cobra which I slew with a stone. But I got so mixed up with the sequence of events that my story never really took off. And Minu's talents were not confined to story telling, though later on he wrote a very readable book called *The Call of the Tiger.* He developed into a good artist, and also acquired a very fine base baritone singing voice which he modelled on Paul Robeson. Later, we joined the army during the War; he stayed on to make it a career, whereas I left.

Minu and I launched into a disgusting career as killers at around the same time. His mother bought him an air gun firing lead shot with a pump action, whereas I acquired a single-shot Daisy air gun, which

I later changed for a Diana which fired a mysterious projectile called
·177 bore pellets. I also recall that Mrs Ismail was wisely parsimonious
with her handout of eight round shots per day, whereas my mother
did not bother to ration the murderous slugs with which I sallied forth.
Thus armed, we started our respective careers as bloodthirsty and
murderous urchins with an innate desire to slaughter anything in
sight. Minu was probably less prodigal than I, perhaps not so much
by inclination as by necessity induced by his mother's policy of
rationing, but I used to search the walls for geckos to be slaughtered.
I would then visit pools of water where frogs lay with legs stretched
and their eyes prominently sticking out of the water like minute
hippopotami. These amphibians were more difficult to account for as
they presented a smaller target and were liable to disappear under
water when slightly wounded. However, when they were well and
truly shot they floated belly up in the water, at which I abandoned
them. I also tried to kill fish, in the shape of small tiddlers which
frequented ponds after the monsoon, but they were more elusive as
they swam mostly under water, and I do not recall being successful
with them. With all this practice I developed into a deadly little killer,
and in retrospect it seems rather odd that my parents did nothing to
deter me from all the cruel and needless massacre that I made a habit
of indulging in. The ponds were full of frogs lying upside down, some
with their entrails hanging out, and the floors often lined with dead
geckos which had been blasted off the walls. My brother never
displayed this compulsive instinct for slaughter, and I can only conjecture that he had wider interests and more satisfying talents which
prevented him from indulging in these mindless orgies of destruction
to prove himself

In the evenings, when lessons were over and I had finished my
death-dealing prowls in the suburbs of the Special Manager's large
bungalow, I would go over to where Minu lived. After he collected
his ration of eight round shots from Mrs Ismail we would make tracks
for the Balrampur zoo, known as Anandbagh. It was small but well
looked-after by Babu Ram Lochan whom we insolently called
'Bauran' (Mad) Lochan. The large mammals were presided ever by
Prince, a fine and friendly tiger, and Bismarck, an aged and excep-
tionally good-looking lion, and consisted of sloth bears, Himalayan
bears, leopards, hyenas, etc. The zoo also acquired an orang-utan
who became a great favourite with visitors. At the entrance was a
museum, which had the skeleton of Chand Murat, an elephant who
was reputedly 11 feet 6 inches at the shoulder, among its prominent
exhibits. Unfortunately, new weights and measures have now been

adopted, to render old records seemingly inconsequential, but certainly this measurement is a record for the Indian elephant.

What Ram Lochan thought of the frequent visits of two evil little boys armed with air guns is not on record, but it could not have been complimentary. Nevertheless, he did not take the matter of our misdemeanours to my father, for I suppose he imagined that animals were there for entertainment, and if it amused the scion of the boss to pepper the animals in his charge with lead shot, it was not his place to object.

Once we entered the portals of the zoo the inmates, with the instinctive perception of wild animals for unpleasant phenomena, seemed to become conscious of a prevalent miasma. An eerie and expectant silence descended on the 'Garden of Tranquillity', or at least so it appears in retrospect. The lion and tigers were immune to our intentions, maybe because they were in large cages, or perhaps because we realized that an assault on these powerful animals would not be tolerated, or maybe their personalities were too strong for our sneaky little minds; but one particular leopard in a small cage was a selected victim. He would start snarling the moment he heard us, and the skin of his tail was raw with the frenzy and hate with which he lashed it on the cement floor. However, he was soon dead with the amount of lead we pumped into him, a monument to the activities of a couple of idiotic boys. The next in line was the flamingo, which we lamed merely because we always found it standing on one leg and wondered what it would do if it lost the use of that leg. Thereafter, we shot at pond herons, egrets, doves and whatever we could find. Luckily, these battues were restrained somewhat by Minu's lack of ammunition, but I continued to shoot at everything in sight. I was specially keen on slaughtering something I had not shot before, and I recall that, after having dropped my first spotted owlet, I reversed my firearm and, resting my folded arms on the butt, closed my eyes and said a short prayer of thanksgiving though I do not recall to what deity. When I opened my eyes the owlet had flown away. Though furious then at the futility of prayer, as I write I cannot but feel elated at my discomfiture. The next incident was when my father discovered me putting boot polish on the wing of a purple sunbird which I had maimed. He rightly confiscated my airgun for some time. Larger birds were of course out of my range with the weaponry I had, and my best efforts in those days was to drop a Brahminy kite, one of the weakest birds of prey.

The erstwhile estate of Balrampur was in the district of Gonda, one of the 48 districts in the United Provinces. There are now over 60 in the State of Uttar Pradesh. Balrampur was 26 miles from the head-quarter city of Gonda by road or rail, and whereas the car journey took one hour, the timings of the rail journey were usually erratic, subject at times to the whim and fancy of the engine driver, who might on considerations stop the train to allow a pot shot at some animal. During the course of the road journey we crossed over the Kuana river. Both banks of the Kuana were forested by miscellaneous and timber trees, with cane brake lining the stream. It was not only picturesque, but had plenty of fish and marsh crocodile. There were many game animals like pig, chital, barking deer that lived off the crops planted by cultivators, and a few leopards. Once a tigress strayed into the jungle from some outlying forest, and I recall my father took great pleasure in destroying it, with great danger to himself, he claimed. As the Kuana jungles were only five miles from Balrampur, it was a favourite picnic spot, where we also went for drives by car or had beats in pursuit of the local fauna.

Further north stretched the great forests of the Bhabar and Tarai from the boundaries of the kingdoms of Bhutan, Sikkim and Nepal, into the Indian mountain system of Naini Tal, Almora and Garhwal. We crossed the Rapti at Bijlipur, three miles from Balrampur, over a pontoon bridge, from where we would often see marsh crocodile and gharial lying on the sandbanks with their mouths open, absorbing the solar heat. These great saurians, relics of a bygone age, often attained great size; the crocodile could grow up to fourteen feet, whereas the slender-snouted gharial or fish-eating crocodile went up to twenty-five feet. The adult male gharial is distinguished by a large protu-berance on its snout, like a *ghara* or earthenware *chatty*, from which it derives its name, and the *ghara* is perhaps used at breeding time to enhance the resonance of a mating call—but I am not sure if this is the reason for the distinguishing feature. In any case, a large male gharial was a most impressive sight lying over 21½ feet off the ground. Crocodilians are supposed to live to great ages, and it is reputed that the sacred crocodiles of the Nile were two hundred years old.

Having crossed over at Bijlipur we arrived at the metre gauge railway station of Kauwapur, 'the Colony of Crows'. The next station was Tulsipur, from where we turned north, though the Estate bound-ary extended to the next station of Pachperwa and the forest block of Chandanpur, with an intermediate station by the name of Gaensari (Rotten Cow), the eastern limit of the Balrampur Raj. From Chandan-pur the forest blocks to the west were Jarwa-Jankpur, Sungarha,

Nandmehra, Bankatwa, Pipra, Sohelwa and Bachkahil, beyond which was the district of Bahraich. Bankatwa was at the centre of the stretch of Balrampur Forest, and had an elaborate Forest Rest House owned by the Estate, picturesquely situated as we entered the forest. From there on the forests were in two sections: the zamindari or Estate-owned forests, which consisted mainly of miscellaneous timber of little value, and which were bounded latitudinally along an east-west axis; and further to the north, and abutted by the Nepal forests, the institutionalized government forests, consisting mainly of the valuable Sal (*Shorea Robusta*), which was in demand for railway fish plates, girders, rafters, door frames and other durables. The policy was to give forests of no great commercial value to the native rulers who could amuse themselves with the sport of shooting, whereas the really valuable forests were retained by the government. The Zamindari forests had cultivation next to them and contained all the '*Chota shikar*' of prolific ungulate species like the chital and pig, that depended on farmers' crops. They also had good resident populations of leopards, but the tigers confined themselves to government forests, in which the main prey species were the solitary Sambhar and the barking deer; the latter is too small to qualify as a favoured prey species, but it shows the lengths to which the tiger went to avoid the human presence, even though plentiful prey was available in Zamindari forests.

My father was thirty-four years old when he arrived in Balrampur, and though he had never gone in for any big game shooting until then, it was not long before he succumbed to the so-called thrill of killing. Shooting was the recognized form of recreation for the Manager of properties situated on the fringes of the forest, and opportunity was provided when he had to inspect the Estate forests.

There was a Forest Officer named Ram Narain Joshi, who had once been a Range Officer in government service; he had served under a British officer called Dunbar Brander, a distinguished zoologist who wrote an authoritative book called *Wild Animals in Central India*, and after whom the hard ground swampdeer has been named *Cervus Duvauceli Branderi*. Joshi related that the local staff called Brander Danda Mar Bandar, or one who hits a monkey with a cudgel, on account of his acerbic nature; and if after a morning's tour Brander thought he had not covered sufficient distance to justify his travelling allowance, he would get into his car and drive round and round the Rest House until he felt he had done the requisite mileage. Old man Joshi was also a progressive character; from being a staunch and caste-bound Brahmin, under the influence of my father and mother he started drinking whisky and eating meat, and brought his wife out of purdah.

Unfortunately, Joshi's daughter, Lachchmi, did not appear to be interested in me, and for a long while I cherished an unrequited regard for her charms. She had a cousin whom we unkindly called Tauwa because of his dark complexion and a lisp which made him mispronounce *kauwa*. Tauwa was a tough little character who would not kowtow to us older boys, and one day after an incident which we thought showed his overweening defiance, we tied him upside down to an overhanging branch of a tree. The plucky boy would not give in, and it was only the appearance of my father, who rode up on his polo pony after my sister complained to him, that saved Tauwa from possible injury. Many years later, when I met Tauwa on his retirement from the army after World War II, we laughed over the occurrence. Needless to say, Lachchmi was greatly incensed, and would not speak to me for several days. After we left Balrampur, Joshi died, ironically of cirhossis of the liver; Lachchmi married one of her clan and had numerous children, and my first bout of calf love was followed by numerous other fruitless affairs.

Father acquired a ·500 Black Powder Express rifle from the Estate armoury. This was an ancient weapon even in those days, a hammer rifle with an underlever action to activate the breech, and fired two different bullets. Though not a very slick-looking weapon, father became a very good shot, and killed four tigers with this rifle until he called a halt to such killing. All his tigers were shot in the government forests, except for the tigress in the Kuana jungles. I used to accompany him on most of his shoots, and got to know the different forests well. I too acquired a knowledge of the ways of shikar and the expertise required to kill animals.

The Estate maintained a number of professional shikaris who were given land in peripheral villages, and were on call when required for tracking, arranging beats, tying machans and other paraphernalia connected with shooting. Needless to say, I envied them their way of life, which I imagined was one long shikar. Feudal States which had forests used so-called sport hunting or shikar for their own recreation, as well as to oblige visiting dignitaries. The more plentiful the game animals, the more often were the States visited, and conservation was the vogue basically because the rulers wanted more to kill.

The shikaris of the Balrampur Raj were a special breed. They had been given land next to the forest, and spent their time either protecting their crops from ungulates, or encompassing the destruction of carnivora. There was Ram Autar, a Pasi or Criminal Tribal by caste, with a great spade-like black beard streaked with grey. His presence was always accompanied by the smell of stale sweat and ganja or marijuana, which he smoked because he claimed that it enabled him to work longer hours in the heat. The Pasi were also intemperate; when at the end of a shoot my father gave them liquor in celebration, not one got home and all slept in the fields.

One day Ram Autar reported to my father that he had seen the tracks of a giant hominid in a nala, where it debouched from the Nepal hills. He also claimed that he had heard an unearthly scream in the vicinity. Having just finished reading a gruesome and disgusting book, *The Gorilla Hunters* by R.M. Ballantine, my imagination was fired, and we went down to the site in the evening. The great waterway from where it led down from a ravine in the Nepal hills was dry, except for stray pools trapped amidst sandstone boulders, but remnants of upturned roots indicated the fury of the flash floods which had occurred during the monsoon. Dense forests lined the bed of the nala and, as we made our ways under the suspended lianas hanging like great serpents, I had a vision of one of us being drawn struggling into the trees. The tracks looked human and were very large, and the absence of an overlap seemed to confirm that they were not those of a four-legged animal. The only animal which could have made those tracks was a bear, and as the place was adjoining the hills, a Himalayan bear could have temporarily strayed down; a large sloth bear can stand seven feet tall. The front feet of a bear are digitigrade, i.e., it walks on the ball of its feet; only the hind paws are plantigrade, and it was probable that there was a complete overlap. Surprisingly, a tracker of the calibre of Ram Autar was caught on the wrong foot. He was probably overawed by the out-size tracks. Or perhaps a Yeti had strayed down from its mountain fastness! Excitement gradually subsided, and was partially revived when Raghubar Dayal, who was carrying my father's loaded ·500 Express and had cocked a hammer against possible eventualities, inadvertently jerked a trigger. There was a loud explosion, and the firearm appeared to leap from 'Garbar' Dayal's grasp, as he was knocked down by the force of the black powder recoil. The huge tracks and the wild screams were forgotten for the moment.

Further to the east, the shikaris were Tharus. They are a simple and honest people, with a delightful sense of fun and a complete disregard for authority. A story is related how one day, when Sir John Hewitt, the Governor of U.P., was guest of honour in a tiger beat, he was attacked by a swarm of bees, and he and his companion took shelter in a cave. At the end of the beat consternation reigned when an empty machan was discovered, and the beaters were deputed to search. As the day got hotter, the trackers were wearying of searching for a missing Governor; before long one of the beaters passed the cave where Hewitt was hiding and called loudly '*Ohh Latia, Ohh Latia!*' (*Lat Sahib* being the common form of address for the Governor) '*Ka jane kahan sar salah lukan hai*' ('I wonder where my sister's husband is hiding'—in Hindu society you can abuse your sister's husband, and he is not supposed to retaliate in kind). But lesser luminaries on the Governor's staff could not tolerate this abuse of godhead, and emerged to haul the poor Tharu over the coals. However, after the shoot, when country liquor was distributed to the Tharu shikaris, they had the last laugh by depicting scenes of hunters who had distinguished themselves in various ways. Among other scenes, there was one about a Mr Dampier ICS ('Damphi Sahib'), erstwhile Deputy Commissioner of Gonda. His elephant was once charged by a wounded tiger, whereupon he got so alarmed that he urinated freely. The scene was depicted by the tiger—a man on all fours with a long tail of grass running at Damphi Sahib on his elephant—another man on all fours. The finale was Damphi pouring water out of a container. However, when sufficient liquor had been consumed, the container was discarded and the entire event enacted more realistically. It was all in fun, and no offence was taken even by the man acting the part of the soaked elephant.

The 'Charkosia Jhari' or eight-mile forest of Nepal consists of the detritus washed down from the Churia Range by the monsoon. Huge boulders of sandstone lie in shallow river beds, subject to sudden flash floods during the rains. Known as the Bhabar in India, these shallow soils merge into the water-logged forests of the terai to form the landscape along the entire Indo-Nepal border. Thanks to processes of land reclamation for agriculture and siltation caused by over-felling, a great deal of the fertile tarai belt as such has disappeared. The Balrampur forests consisted largely of the Bhabar, and it was here that a self-imposed barrier on tiger habitat was voluntarily maintained which was seldom trespassed. Known habitat niches were invariably occupied, and if a tiger occupying a certain habitat was shot he was soon replaced by some kind of communication within the tiger population building up in Nepal. I recall Sanwar Bhanwar, a favourite tiger beat in the Bankatwa jungles, a wild forest block intersected by deep ravines, which was immediately replaced, but beyond which there was no encroachment; no sooner had my father slaughtered a large tiger with his hammer ·500 Express than another one appeared. The same system applied to the forest block of Bachkahi, where a ravine led down from the abutting mountain and was seemingly equipped with a kind of stop-valve which only allowed a replacement when required. The Balrampur shikaris were well aware of this selective occupation by tigers, and they were, of course, the ultimate aim of every so-called hunter. No firearms were supposed to be fired within two miles of a forest patch which supposedly held a tiger, and during such a beat no one could shoot at any other animal. Further down, however, there were general beats in which other game animals could be shot subject to size regulations. These beats might produce sloth bears, leopards, and the numerous ungulates which preyed upon the cultivators' fields, but never tigers.

My brother Jumper was just as keen as I was on our trips to the great forests, for which the Raj was famous. The Estate motor garage was equipped with a number of vehicles, from which my father had a selection when he went on tour. There was a Buick, which was usually ridden by the minor Maharaja, Pateshwari Prasad Singh, his uncle Girdhari Singh and the driver Ram Das. Apart from this car, we could choose any other, and the choice, influenced by our liking for the driver, was usually made by Jumper and me, of course with the concurrence of Father. There was Mohammed Hussain who, together with Ram Das, was the best driver. The former was very keen on the jungles, and was always ready to 'halaal', or slit the throat, of an edible animal shot in a beat, after a suitable invocation to Allah to make the flesh consumable by a progeny of the faithful. Apart from being fearless, he did not have any compunction in cutting the throat of a dead animal in a token gesture; he was thus popular and able to provide the Muslim staff with meat without unnecessary qualms. However, one day he nearly met his nemesis: as he was 'halaaling' a spotted deer which Father had shot, three sloth bears appeared within a few yards. These bears have the reputation of being exceedingly fierce, and Hussain did not wait upon the order of his going. He had a penchant for swear words, which he gave vent to irrespective of the quality of his audience, and Mother who was sitting with me and

Father on the machan, now had the opportunity of listening to some
choice invectives regarding the bears' relatives as Hussain fled breath-
lessly to shin up a tree with great agility.

Our favourite driver, however, was Bechan, who looked like a dark
and rather shop-soiled edition of Clark Gable. He was the chauffeur
of an ancient off-white Cadillac fitted with a searchlight, which he
manipulated with great dexterity while driving the vehicle along
bullock cart tracks and avoiding trees standing in his line of advance.
He had wonderful eyesight, and we often drove into the forest at night
looking for animals to shoot. He would spot eyes reflected by the
searchlight at incredible distances, and had worked out through
experience that the eyes of tigers shone like bright electric bulbs, but
shone green at angles. Leopards were a smaller edition. Bears, with
their weak eyesight, shone red. Spotted deer were pin-point, and
were usually in large groups, and so on down the line. Unfortunately,
we encouraged him in these pursuits and I cannot blame him for
falling in with our wishes. As my father was the chief executive and
the forests belonged to the Estate, no one could query the complete
disregard of any rules of sportsmanship written or unwritten. Our
selectivity was only observed when there was the question of the
relative dimensions of the trophy, but we had to kill, and it did not
matter how many animals escaped wounded on dark nights.

One night we were returning to camp when we saw a hyena and
promptly let fly. As everyone was firing from the moving vehicle we
ran out of ammunition and decided to run the poor hyena over with
the Cadillac to put him out of his misery. He would not die, and
eventually we left the suffering beast, after repeated efforts to kill him,
to be collected in the morning. As I consider in retrospect the brutality
and the callousness which we indulged in, I can only deeply regret
the suffering that the human has inflicted on the animal, for like me
there have been many millions of so-called sportsmen. I wonder what
the line up will be on the day of reckoning.

As I graduated towards the killing of bigger animals the quality of
firearms assumed greater importance. Minu and I acquired a catalogue of rifle ballistics, and we carefully studied the details of muzzle
velocity in feet per second and muzzle energy in foot pounds. I still
remember that the American 30·06 calibre fired four weights of bullet
of 220, 180, 150 and 110 grains, and the 110 grain bullet with a velocity
of 3,500 feet per second was only approached by the 250/3,000
Savage which had a muzzle velocity of 3,150; the ·280 Ross rifle was
perhaps third with 2,800. Velocity fell with the weight of bullets, as

the muzzle energy in foot-pounds increased. The choice rifles were the King Ejectors in the shape of the Double Barrel Magnum made by Holland & Holland of ·375 and ·465 bore, and were status symbols which every so-called hunter had to possess. All these firearms were powered by cordite. The relatively obsolescent ·500 Black Powder Express used by Father had a velocity of just over 1,000 and a muzzle energy of under 2,000 foot-pounds compared with the over-5,000 ft lbs of the bigger bores. There was a ·577 Black Powder which was a larger edition of the ·500, and there is a record of a ·600 which was used as an anti-tank weapon in World War I. Interestingly enough, that was the weapon used by A.W. Strachan, a police officer who lost his leg after being mauled by a tigress. It fired a 700 grain bullet with a velocity of 1,950 and an energy of 7,600 foot-pounds. More recently, a ·700 Nitre Express has been built for an American millionaire by Holland & Holland. Weighing nineteen pounds to even the recoil, it hurls a projectile with a muzzle energy of over 9,000 foot-pounds and costs £ 50,000. With the present plight of endangered species, is this manufacture a gimmick, an eccentricity, or a tribute to the four thousand elephants to be culled in Zimbabwe by wildlife experts?

Minu and I used to discuss with enormous gravity the use of heavy bores versus light rifles. The big rifles had such massive recoils that firing more than a few shots was not only unpleasant but dangerous. The choice of sophisticated weaponry became an exalted crutch for the egotistical destruction of the biggest and the strongest, and even the so-called pleasure of the chase was sacrificed to the efficacy of the kill.

In 1924 my sister Amar was born in Naini Tal, where Balrampur had properties. And a brother, Balram, was born in 1926 in Balrampur, from where he derived his name. Later that year, Jumper was to be sent to the Prince of Wales Royal Indian Military College in Dehra Dun. He never had the thirst for blood which had appeared in my genes, and started off with a love of animals inherited from Mother. He kept different varieties of pigeons in the loft at our home. There were the pouters, the homing pigeons and the one which looped the loop. He watched them endlessly as they flew into the skies, as they fought for dominance challenging other males with throaty cooing. However, he encouraged cockfights, and at the zoo we watched the great Rhode Island Reds and Leg Horns put to flight by the tiny bantams from the forests. We listened to the music in the lilting clarion of the jungle cocks, which transported us back to the wondrous land they came from.

Jumper and I had been tutored at home by a series of governesses, who found our escapades, especially those of my quick-silver brother, bothersome. There was an American, Miss Bayles, who never tired of telling us what a wonderful country America was, and complaining of the monotony of our food. She soon returned to the country she was so enamoured of, after complaining that her ked-geree had been obtained from the sweeper. She was replaced by a Miss Anderson from Scotland, a desiccated and cadaverous lady, of an unbelievable thinness and with a parchment complexion. However, we got on well with her and she had no major complaints until we decided her single dimension simply could not be real, and we had to see her without any clothes on. We bided our time until, one morning, we burst into the toilet where she was having a tub bath. She gave an outraged shriek as she grabbed her towel to conceal her modesty from two impish boys staring in disbelief at her slender proportions. Archimedes' Principle of Displacement seemed scarcely vindicated in the full tub as she leapt out with incredible agility, without a ripple but also without the triumphant 'Eureka'. Needless to say, she submitted her resignation to our irate mother whose apologetic plea that 'boys will be boys' was of no avail. We then got a Mr Ram Chandra Joshi from the Naini Tal hills, but by that time Jumper was due for the RIMC.

Father escorted him to Dehra Dun, and on his return described how he had left a small figure forlornly fighting back his tears on the school playground. He was only eleven years old, but a number of Sikhs with full-blown beards were his class fellows. However, Jumper was soon enjoying himself at a school which was out of a *Boys Own* advertisement. There was a Sergt-Major Gorman who had been the Heavyweight army boxing champion. There was Sergt-Major Murphy, a Lightweight champion; and F.C. Wood, who had played rugger for England, was his House Master. That summer we went to Mussoorie, fourteen miles up the hill from Dehra Dun, where one of the attractions was that Jumper would be representing the RIMC against a local Anglo-Indian school. We stayed at the Savoy Hotel, and I recall the night of our journey to the skating rink where the boxing was taking place. I was picked up in what was the normal mode of transport in hill stations, a double rickshaw pulled by a team of 4–6 coolies known as Jhampanies. I rode in a rickshaw with Maharajkumar Mahijit Singh of Kapurthala, the second son of the Maharaja. Commonly known as

Midget, he was a bluff, genial man about town, and a great ladies' man. He was accompanied by Rita Parr, a cabaret artist in an expensive fur coat, and I still recall wondering why he was holding her hand. Jumper, fighting at Pin weight, lost by one point to P. Monier, who was ever so much taller, but each of his admiring family was full of praise for his plucky display.

Midget was looking after the U.P. property of Kapurthala, which had previously been managed by my grandfather, and included the Ikauna forests in Bahraich, a district next to Gonda. Our uncle Maharaj Singh happened to be the Deputy Commissioner of Bahraich. Midget was a very convivial type, and fond of liquor, and he and Father got on very well. He often visited us at Balrampur, and one Christmas he brought a man called Keelan, the Agent or head of the local metre gauge railway of the Bengal and North-Western Railway, to Bankatwa. He was armed with a very slick double-barrel rifle of a lesser-known bore, ·333, with which he scored a right and a left at sambhar stags at long distances, and for a time this became our favourite weapon. We also queued up to sit on a machan with him as he used to teach us how to cut figures in leaves with a penknife, which was great fun, whereas other shikaris told us to keep quiet and glared at us if we dared move. However, Keelan's ·333 was soon forgotten once we saw the Double Ejector Holland & Holland ·465 and ·375 Magnums belonging to Midget, of whom we were very fond.

Despite having such an exquisite selection of firearms, Midget was an execrable shot. He would bring along a timber contractor called Ikram Hussain, supposed to be an excellent marksman, as a backup gun. During one beat at Sohelwa, Father had read the previous day in a book by Colonel A.E. Stewart that in a tiger beat it was advisable to have a machan with a reliable rifle behind the normal line in case a tiger was wounded. As a result, a machan was put up behind the one occupied by Midget and Ikram. Father and I occupied another one. A tigress appeared before our machan and Father let her go in front of Midget, who fired a shot backed up by Ikram. The tigress grunted, and raced off in great leaps towards the rear machan which was occupied by Lala Babu, one of my heroes and an excellent rifle shot. He dropped her in full stride, and if it had not been for his fortuitous positioning, the tigress would have got away. The trophy was awarded to Midget according to the unwritten rule that he had drawn first blood. Ikram's shot was presumed to have gone wide, and I was thrilled that my champion had scored a bulls eye whereas the shikari from Bahraich, an ugly pockmarked man, had missed a standing shot. Midget stayed on with us a few days and refereed a cricket match in which Jumper and I played Maharaj Singh's two sons. He left after awarding a prize of half a rupee.

Lala Babu was a redoubtable man, and the owner of a village in the heart of the forest. He was the Superintendent of the *Filkhana* or elephant stable at Sunderbagh belonging to the Estate, which consisted of fifty elephants. Many of these were outsize males, and notoriously difficult to handle when in 'Musth', a seasonal mental disorder prevalent among tuskers. This disorder,which has not been fully explained, is thought to be connected with a sexual derangement. The outward manifestation is an oily discharge from two orifices close to the tusker's temples. The tusker then becomes aggressive and impossible to handle. The first hate is the *Filwan* or mahawat, and he has to quickly tether the elephant before losing control, otherwise no one else can control the tusker. The only man the tusker will tolerate is the bhishti or waterman, and the female who brings his rations, and he has to be tethered throughout the 'Musth' period. Depending on who approaches, the tusker will strain at his shackles, and hurl branches for long distances at the bystander. Subject to the maturity and size of the elephant, the condition may last for many months, and at Balrampur these big tuskers were only used on ceremonial occasions, and even then subject to their being manageable, which the *Filwans* attempted to ensure by the administration of traditional herbal tranquillizers.

Lala Babu claimed that one could become a crack shot only after having expended a bullock-cart load of empties. Whether he had done so or not I am unable to bear witness, but I cannot recall his having missed a four-legged animal. One day he shot a chital at 500 yards. I used to enjoy his late evening meetings with the shikaris. There were Ram Autar and Sheo Lal, the top men of their profession. There was Sheo Charan, and Moosey or Rat, who was supposed to have crawled down a large hole after a wounded bear and thereby earned his nickname. There were Goga and Biraji the Tharus, and many more. Lala Babu would sit smoking his hookah filled with 'khamira' or scented tobacco, while the shikaris sat around and outlined the next day's programme. It was always an experience to sit with Lal Bhalo as there was a professional touch to what he did while on shikar. He had an exquisite 450/400 double-barrel rifle, with engravings on the breech, which chambered two business-like metal cartridges. His usual companion was his supposed grandson, a pudding faced little boy called Rama, though no one was aware of his father as he never did appear during the almost ten years I was there. Rama would sit unobtrusively behind his grandmother picking his nose. Uncharitably, we used to discuss as to what he did with the proceeds of his excavations, but there was never any tangible proof.

Lala Babu had been very keen on wrestling in his younger days, and under the guidance of Father a great wrestling 'dangal' or Meet was held, to which the top wrestlers of the country would be invited. Though the great Gama never came, his brother Imam Baksh, who some claimed was even better than Gama, came one year. Also Kikkar Singh, the Sikh wrestler whom confreres claimed was so strong that he could pull out a Babul (*Acacia Arabica*) by the roots. Chota Gama came with Hameeda, who later became the top wrestler in India. Among lesser-known luminaries there were Ismail Bechain, Aziz Memna, the Chaubeys from Mathura who were so large that no one could turn them over to put them on their backs, and the Bairagi or singing priests from Ayodhya, the birthplace of Ram. There was Nawab Pahlwan, the handsome wrestler from Lahore, who funked fighting Hameeda, and was never the same champion after doing so. And many more. They were all paid cash prizes and were given brightly embroidered turbans and scarves, and the fame of these contests spread far and wide. Father had an Akhara (or wrestling pit) dug in our house, and we were encouraged to wrestle every morning, supervised by Sarwar Khan who was the *Filwan* in charge of Frank Bahadur of the Balrampur elephants. The patron saint of wrestling was supposed to be Ali, the son of the prophet Mohammed, and before grappling we were expected to throw earth on a small gar-landed accumulation of earth known as Ali's Mound.

During his holidays from the RIMC my brother stayed with Father in Balrampur while Mother took me and the two younger children to Naini Tal. Jumper had built up a reputation for intrepidity when he gave chase on his bicycle to a runaway horse pulling an 'ekka', thus rescuing an old and wailing woman. He wrestled with Faujdar Khan, son of Sarwar Khan, and played polo with my father, Gilan, and 'Pinchin', an ex-soldier who had been taken on as Superintendent of Gardens by the father of the then Maharaja, Bhagwati Prasad. Pinchins' real name was A.E. Shenton; he had been a professional footballer, and played for the Everton First Division side before joining the army and coming out to India with the East Surrey Regiment if my memory serves me. The Maharaja saw him playing at Naini Tal and, impressed by his performance, offered him the job of looking after the gardens of the Estate. A more lovable man never lived, and he was unfortunate in that he married an Anglo-Indian woman who took up with a man called Lancaster who owned a motor shop in Lucknow. She was thoroughly unfaithful to Pinchin, and his life was sorrowed by numerous children who all bore his name, but of whose paternity he was doubtful.

Jaswant was doing very well at school, especially at games, and was single-minded about joining the army, and for which purpcse the RIMC provided special training. Meanwhile, I had had a very sickly childhood, and was educated at home. From the age of three to eight I was constantly ill, and despite prolonged treatment, no improvement took place. I remember Mother trying to persuade me to drink quail soup, which was in fact warm water flavoured with a nausea preventive, which I brought up immediately. When all hope appeared to have ended, a Colonel Hunter, the Civil Surgeon at Naini Tal, prescribed a pill called Parathyroid which he said without much enthusiasm 'could do no harm'. With that administration I never looked back, and it apparently transpired that my system lacked calcium. For this early setback I blame my late development in life, for though I loved my elder brother dearly I have always been envious of his prowess at games, and his extroverted enthusiasm for life. If war years had not intervened he would have represented India in at least one of the team games he was so good at.

After Jumper returned to school, Father came up to Naini Tal. We lived in Jubilee Hall, probably the highest house in the hills of Naini Tal. Father was a very good tennis player, and had won the All India Doubles Championship two years running. Though happily married, he had a keen eye for the girls, and always chose his Mixed Doubles partners with perception. Violet Persee (née Blunt) was not only a good tennis player with whom he won the event, but also one of the many women I fell in love with. When in later years I saw her, after she had put on a lot of weight, I wondered why. Phyll Osmaston was hopeless at tennis, but Father claimed it did not matter as she was so good looking. Edith Roe was mediocre in looks as well as tennis, and we teased her by repeating Idi Idi-otic ad infinitum. It was at the Metropole Hotel, where the tennis tournament took place, that we met the legendary Jim Corbett who lived at Gurney House, higher up on the same hill. He used to came to watch the tennis and I recall this shy man unobtrusively walking down the hill from a secluded corner. Needless to say, I immediately appropriated him, and he did not know what he was letting himself in for when he suggested that I come and visit him every Sunday morning. Come hell or high water, I would get to Gurney House, where I met his half sister Mary Doyle, his sister Maggie, and Robin the Cocker whom Corbett made famous in his writings. He once took my father up the hill to climb a pine tree, from which they swung to the top of a plateau. He also took him on a goat path up the steep hill of Deopata. Later, my father took me on the walk; I nearly died of fright looking down into the yawning abyss below. Corbett taught me how to catch a porcupine in a gin trap; it used to ravage our potato crop. One day he came to invite me to accompany him on a hunt of the biggest leopard in all the hills, but unfortunately I was out. We met often at the Chalet, where government officials acted Gilbert and Sullivan plays. I recall the great pleasure with which we watched these amateur performances. Later, I went to school in Jim's *alma mater*, Philander Smith College. During the war years he trained the Indian Army in jungle warfare while I followed a brief and undistinguished war career with the Gunners. I met Corbett before he departed for Kenya in 1947. His last offer was that I take over his farm in Tanganyika, where he was the youngest of three bachelor partners.

I have sometimes read of the halcyon years of a person's life, and I feel our Balrampur years could qualify for that appellation as far as I am concerned. Father and Mother were married at the age of twenty-five. People should have their families when they are young enough to grow up with their children, and Father and Mother were persons we looked up to as companions as well as parents. Mother and Father were entirely suited to each other, and in Balrampur were loved and respected by all. My brother and I would, as a ritual, sit with Father when he had a tub bath in the morning, and discuss all sorts of matters. He related how, when on holiday as an undergraduate in Oxford, he went to the Vatican and heard 'San Carlo Boromio, Ora Pro Nobis' being chanted in praise of the Pope. The nearest Father could get to the rhythm of this chant was via an old music hall ditty, 'O Judy O' Grady, my bonnie bride . . . ', which he sang with such gusto that the Pope was moved to enquire about the identity of the *basso profundo* who chanted his praises! In the evenings Father sang to us, and we loved the Negro spirituals made famous by Paul Robeson, whose singing voice his own so closely resembled. Three decades later the songs still bring a nostalgia for those far off days.

Balrampur was a small kingdom on its own, and Father was king there by proxy. It had an army of about 300 soldiers commanded by an ex-serviceman of the erstwhile Indian regiment of the Third Brahmins, with the honorific rank of Brigadier and named Mata Din Tiwari, a stalwart over six feet tall. There was a platoon of Gurkhas with Havaldar Puran Bahadur Thapa in command, and a contingent of cavalry commanded by Risaldar Mohammad Qifiyat Khan, who had won the Indian Order of Merit, the equivalent of the Victoria

Cross for Indians in World War I. There were Havaldar Ghulam
Mohammed Tiwana and his brother, a rough rider who trained the
horses. It was a romantic period. We played tennis at the Estate Guest
House, where Mother, who had no eye for ball games, played a Mrs
Williams, who served underhand, and was the only person she could
defeat. She looked after the Maharajas' sisters and was a trained nurse.
There was in charge of the Estate Hospital a Dr Ram Charan Bud-
haolia, a short, rotund little man with fierce-looking waxed mous-
taches, and a dozen offspring. There was Miss Mendies, the lady
doctor, who was large, dark and unattractive; in a crisis of hopeless
depression after no one sought her hand in marriage, she adopted a
son called Ronnie. Ronnie was the same age as my younger brother
and sister and claimed that his running ability was due to a plentiful
consumption of nasal produce. He encouraged my brother and sister
to emulate the means of his prowess, but whether due to insufficient
production or lack of single-minded dedication, Ronnie Mendies,
with his natural supply of anabolic steroids, always led the field.

Father and Mother had annual Christmas camps at Bankatwa or
Chandanpur, where Grandfather, Raja Sir Harnam Singh, came with
our Uncles—Dalip Singh, a brilliant lawyer in Lahore and later a Judge
in the High Court; Lt Col. Shumsher Singh or Shummy, who had
played cricket for Kent—and our only Aunt, Amrit, who had been
Head Girl at Sherborne, and later became Health Minister in independent India. Grandfather was quite a tyrant and all his children
were afraid of his temper. One day the morning paper did not arrive,
and the old man was in a fearsome rage as all the other adults of the
family had gone out shooting. Jumper and I were asked to try and
mollify Grandfather, which we succeeded in doing. We considered
this very cowardly behaviour, but perhaps it was merely diplomacy.

We loved Uncle Dalip, who had been a bachelor till he was over
forty and treated us as if he and we were the same age. Every incident
interested him, and we were always sad when the camp came to an
end, and he left. Mother used to tell us that she nearly married Dalip
before meeting Father. There were innumerable anecdotes about
Uncle Dalip's conduct in the courts of law. As a High Court Judge he
had acquired a reputation for sardonic wit and as a person who did
not suffer fools lightly. Once, while in particularly acerbic humour
during a bench sitting, he periodically murmured or exclaimed
'Rubbish' as a lawyer argued a case. At some stage, after an eloquent
silence, Justice Dalip Singh addressed the court and in thinly veiled
sarcasm said, 'Perhaps the Hon'ble Appellate Lawyer would care to
make a statement'—whereupon the lawyer riposted: 'My Lord, what

is there for me to say, for nothing but "rubbish" comes out of your mouth?' A titter went round the court: the biter had been bit.

Shummy, strangely, was a great coward. He used to shoot a line about his exploits during World War I in East Africa, where he was on medical service, stimulated perhaps by the record of his brother who had won the MC in the same service. We only suspected his cowardice when he insisted on taking his service revolver into the machan during a beat. But one day during a beat a large leopard well known as the Sangipur Leopard appeared where Shummy sat with Mother and Zuhra Ismail. When queried as to why he did not fire at the leopard, Shummy pompously exclaimed, 'How could I, with you girls sitting with me'. In fact he had been too petrified to do anything.

As we have already noted, tigers stayed away from populated areas, but the more adaptable and less demanding leopards were to be found everywhere. Most forest blocks had their prominent leopards, big animals, almost as large as small tigresses: the Gaurmai Leopard, the Pipra Leopard, the Sangipur Leopard, the Ramna Leopard, and many others. Besides sharing ranges, with their unobtrusive life style they find intraspecific coexistence easier than the more demanding and territorially dominating tiger. The leopard can live almost anywhere, in deep forest, in scrubland, and next to villages. His catholicity of demands with regards to prey is wide ranging. His arboreal abilities enable him to live off avian and simian prey. The power and agility of his whipcord muscles place larger prey species within his range, but the fates which plan life schedules have been unkind: his beautiful coat is coveted by humans, and his smartness has earned him an evil reputation.

But the fates were also planning our life schedules. Jumper and I had won accolades in the world of shikar. He had shot a fine leopard measuring seven feet four inches and had a forest road in the Kuana jungles named after him as Jaswant Road. I had shot a leopardess and a tiger, and had a tusker named after me as Arjun Bahadur, whose name belied his cowardly nature. One evening Father sat over a leopard kill. Soon a leopard appeared, followed by a third and a fourth. They snacked and played, while he smoked and fidgeted. He was so overwhelmed by the setting that he returned the old hammer ·500 Express to the armoury, and never picked up a rifle again. He had expiated his crime against the wounded hyena from the off-white Cadillac.

And time was running out. Maharaja Pateshwari Prasad Singh was becoming of marriageable age, yet despite a succession of European tutors and companions he remained *non compos mentis*, and according to record, encouraged by one of his tutors—an outlandish man who went by the name of Captain O'Toole, became impotent through self abuse. However, the Government of U.P. was keen on a dynastic marriage with the daughter of the Commander-in-Chief of Nepal, a good looking and intelligent girl. Father was asked for his concurrence, and when he found himself unable to agree to the immorality of linking the life of a young and beautiful girl to that of an imbecile, he was summarily transferred by orders of the British Governor, Sir Malcolm Hailey. As a postscript, when asked by his sisters as to what he would call his wife, as they would be calling her Bhabi (brother's wife), Pateshwari Prasad replied that he would address her as Bhabi too. We left Balrampur in 1932, and the Gonda railway platform, reputed to be the second longest in India, resounded to the weeping of Father's subordinates: a tremendous tribute.

In Volume II of *The Men Who Ruled India*, Philip Woodruffe mentions a young Englishman in the I.C.S., Hugh Lane, who was sent around 1940 to Lucknow to work under the first Indian Deputy Commissioner there—'Jasbir Singh, a man widely liked and admired.' Woodruffe goes on to quote Lane: 'I was soon an ardent admirer of my D.C., who trusted me with so much and seemed so wise and experienced himself . . . . To me he was always a guide, philosopher and friend, and when he died I felt as though I had lost my own father.' Father lived up to 1945, but the kind of respect and affection shown to him in Balrampur seems to have surrounded him wherever he worked.

2 Interlude

As the metre gauge train steamed out of the long railway platform of Gonda Junction, the usually empty space was thronged with people. People had come to bid us farewell from a distance of twenty-six miles from Balrampur. There was hardly a dry eye in the assemblage, and we were all overwhelmed by the occasion. Even my strong and athletic father was visibly affected on leaving a people he had ruled for ten years, for in those days feudal chieftains were despotic administrators, and Father represented the Maharaja who was a minor.

The Indian in the main is a sentimental person, but there is no doubt that a genuine affection underlay this effusive demonstration at the final parting, and twenty-five years later when we visited Balrampur, when several old timers including Father had passed on, many of those remaining suggested that my brother and I should return to guide their destiny. Almost sixty years later groups from Balrampur, sons and grandsons of the ones I knew, come to visit the Dudhwa National Park and to witness the struggles for a cause of a man who had lived among their forebears.

As I watched through the window of the departing train, there was Kenneth Whiting, the Bandmaster from a British Regiment who, like Pinchin, had married an Anglo-Indian girl, but sired his own offspring and taught uneducated peasants to play 'Loch Lomond' and regimental marches with élan. There was his predecessor, Mr Gade, a withered old Eurasian who thought he had done his patriotic duty by teaching his charges to play 'God Save the King'. There was Butterfield, a gnarled old gentleman who was in charge of the elephant stable, and Dukoff Gordon, an exceedingly dark Anglo-Indian, who was inclined to make out that he was the Duke of Gordon. And Ratan Singh, or Tanna, who had been Mother's jhampani and who was appointed a peon but chose to resign his post to follow our fortunes. My anguish was complete when my old guru, Lala Babu, passed from

my ken, and I saw him returning to his village, in the forest of
Bankatwa, his streamlined 450/500 in hand, with its 3¼-inch cartridge
and engraved chamber.

As the tedious journey drew on, the highlights of the ten halcyon
years passed before me. I recalled listening to records of Enrico
Caruso, the great tenor singing 'On With the Motley', and his heroic
rendition of Mephistopheles in the marvellous quartet from Faust;
hearing about Jack Dempsey, 'The Manassa Mauler', and his two
defeats by the ex-marine Gene Tunney and his refusal to fight the
coloured Harry Wills, 'the Brown Panther'; L'il Arthur, who was hated
by the Whites for being the Champion; Big Bill Tilden and Mme
Lenglen the tennis stars; and Douglas Fairbanks in the *Thief of
Baghdad*, swinging from the chandeliers. I thought of Gertrude
Emerson, a young woman from the United States, who lived for two
years in a remote village in Pachperwa under the aegis of Father and
wrote a book *Voiceless India*. I heard Father singing 'Carry Me Back
to Old Virginny' and 'Ol Man River', in his rolling bass, accompanied
by Mother and a couple of visiting missionaries. I wondered what lay
in the future.

Father had taken no leave during our stay in Balrampur and,
somewhat affected by his abrupt dismissal because his humanitarian
principles were not in keeping with the dynastic ad hocism of his
British employers, he took a year's leave. He resolved to spend this
partially in Simla with his eldest brother, and partly in Lucknow, in a
house which he took on rent. My education was also a consideration,
for hitherto we had a succession of tutors. My childhood had been a
sickly one, which affected my development and made me withdrawn
and introverted. With our departure from Balrampur in 1932, the
situation became complicated thanks to the uncertainty of my parents'
movements, and it was resolved to send me to school as a day scholar.
I was given the choice of going to Bishop Cotton School in Simla,
where I would presumably have stayed with my parents while they
were on leave there, or to Philander Smith College in Naini Tal. I
gathered that Jim Corbett had initially been educated there, and
Busher, the Principal, had been his class fellow. I therefore opted for
PSC, and it was arranged that I would be a paying student in the home
of the Headmaster, one F.G. Brandon. 'Barney', as he was known
behind his back, was a remarkably erudite person who was known
to be a strict disciplinarian. In a school where caning was on the
curriculum, he had the reputation of having a remarkably flexible,
wristy follow through, exceeded only in its effectiveness by Old Man
Busher in his infrequent sallies. Barney had no children, but two

nephews stayed with him and he displayed a human side to his nature when he summoned us in the evening for one hour to practise the yo-yo, the current craze. It was incongruous to watch this scholarly man botch his efforts to make the yo-yo climb the attached string, while three semi-literate urchins stood before him performing all sorts of gyrations with the instrument.

Staying out of school made me a confirmed stranger to the usual PSC activities, and even in the classroom I was in the school, but not of it. In addition, being dominated by Anglo-Indians, PSC was replete with talk of natives, of 'niggers' or 'nigs', and 'home' in England. The darker the complexion, the more vociferous were they in talking of British relations; and one Keelan, darker than any 'nig', delighted in talking of his Scottish descent, and his elegant home in Dhanbad Railway Colony. Though staying with the Headmaster called for a certain reserve when dealing with classmates who were ordinary boarders, I used to regale the other boys with tales of Barney's activities with the yo-yo. Class was fun, especially when one didn't have to pay too much attention to what was put on the blackboard, but we had to be careful of the master who was treated with such cavalier indifference. One James Purves Lochner, whom we called Chench because of the small-pox (*chenchak*) marks on his face, was a compulsive wielder of the cane, and the only one who had not so far felt his whiplash was I. He called upon me to prove a geometric theorem—I think it was No. 5 in Euclid, which concluded: and similarly . . . QED. However, realizing that we learnt our lessons by rote and, hoping to even the score, he insisted on my proving it on the board. A hushed silence fell in the classroom, and as Lochner waggled his cane hopefully, my adrenalin took over. I proved my point and fled from his sadistic proximity still unscathed. However, the boys could be equally nasty, and one morning I discovered to my consternation that they had pinned on the notice board a particularly sloppy letter I had written to a girl in our sister school across the hill.

Staying with the Headmaster was an inducement to study, apart from the fact that I was not good enough at games to represent the school. But its 'A' team was able to challenge the British Army soccer sides and the much larger Catholic school, St Joseph's, at hockey. I built myself a hide in the forest behind Barney's residence to study and, hearing a click of the safety catch one evening, crawled out to look into the twin barrels of old Man Busher's shotgun as he looked for pine martens.

I took upon myself to write a book on shikar, but gave up when I found that all I could manage was a transcription of Dunbar Brander's

Wild Animals of Central India. I hung a pair of sambhar antlers over my bed, and was unpleasantly surprised when they fell off the wall and broke, nearly impaling me in the process.

The year after I passed the Junior Cambridge exam Father was posted to Banaras as Personal Assistant to the Deputy Commissioner. My parents rented a house called Kumaun Lodge below Philander Smith, from where I trudged up to school every morning. My sister and brother also joined the kindergarten class under a Miss Mooney, a powerful and eccentric junior school teacher. Our lunch used to be sent up the hill to be eaten together by the three of us, but Balram and Amar complained to Mother that I was ashamed of them and ate my meal at a distance. One day, while in my classroom at school on the top floor of the school, I looked down to see the whole of the kindergarten trooping out into the open. I was delighted to see the children cropping grass on the hillside. Their formidable teacher had punished them for some misdemeanour and, while the great lammer-geiers quartered the skies above Laria Kanta, my brother and sister chewed grass below!

Jumper fell down at the RIMC and broke his teeth, but I was pleasantly surprised when he came to Naini Tal for a few days' rest. We played football on the tennis court attached to Kumaun Lodge, and the rival teams were made up largely of coolies employed to carry my mother up hill and down dale in the conveyance known as a dandy, which four men carried on their shoulders. Our neighbours were F.W. Champion, a forest officer who became famous as a conservationist and photographer while his compatriots slaughtered tigers. He wrote two outstanding books, *With a Camera in Tigerland* and *The Jungle in Sunlight and Shadow*. Another neighbour was Eric Mobbs, a silviculturist. A peppery man who objected to our searching for a football which had fallen into a crop of stinging nettle in his compound, he attacked me when we were searching for the ball. But, trained as a wrestler at Balrampur, I tripped him into the nettles that he was so solicitous about. As he emerged, his red face swollen and redder for the stings, Sylvia Mobbs shrieked admonishments from below.

I introduced Jumper to 'Gobbo' Gorman, my class-fellow and the son, through a Eurasian woman, of Sgt-Major Gorman, ex-Heavy-weight boxing champion of the British Army and now at the RIMC. 'Gobbo' himself had a formidable punch, and one evening during a fracas at a game of hockey with a local team, he knocked out one of the 'nigs' and broke his nose, which earned him much applause from others of his ilk.

During our holidays we went to Banaras, where Father was posted. I still had an air rifle with which I relentlessly pursued the avian population. Balram acquired a cast-off weapon of mine. One day, he was casually shooting at some goats being grazed by an old woman. He was entertained by the way they flicked their tails when hit. When the woman remonstrated he let fly at her and hit her in the leg. Needless to say, Father was furious and just retribution followed. But generally, Banaras, or Varanasi as it is now known, was a thoroughly depressing, and sordid,city. Known as the sacred city of the Hindus, its burning ghats on the banks of the Ganges are particularly busy. The contract for cremations is with the Dom Raja or head of the clan of Doms, the lowest caste among the Hindus, whose profession it is to burn dead bodies. The Raja was very dark and paunchy, and ate and drank to excess; but he was a multi-millionaire by virtue of his sordid occupation.

The most attractive feature of Banaras was the presence of the Maharajkumar of Vizianagram. His brother was ruler of the State in the South, but 'Vizzy', as he was commonly known, had settled in Banaras. He lived in an elegant palace with a large cricket pitch fashioned on the Oval in England, the entrance to which was guarded by innumerable full-mounted tigers. It was an oasis in the midst of a city of filth, vitiated only by the spectacle of the supplicating jaws of his stuffed tigers. Though heavily in debt, Vizzy was the soul of hospitality, as befitted the scion of a princely clan. While Father and Jumper played cricket, I was given a choice of his select armoury. I was sent on a tiger shoot where, sitting on a machan between two large and protective gentlemen during a beat, I was so squashed that it became impossible to aim my rifle properly. The result was that we only managed to wound the tiger at which all of us had fired simultaneously. We went to Vizzy's shooting block in Imilia, where we drank champagne every evening and father toasted Fizzy Vizzy.

Vizzy was an enthusiastic even if not great cricketer; but he had been under the tutelage of Hobbs and Sutcliffe, two all-time greats in English cricket. While we were in Banaras, Hobbs came out to stay. His record of 196 centuries in first class cricket has never been broken. Shortly afterwards, the MCC cricket team came out to India, and visited Banaras. Led by D.R. Jardine, the controversial captain of bodyline fame in Australia, we watched in fascination as an Indian side captained by Vizzy defeated the British team, the only defeat they sustained in India. Jardine was furious and, greatly incensed by the defeat, was heard to instruct one of his fast bowlers, Nobby Clark, to try some bodyline at the Maharajkumar's bloody head! At a dance that evening, as was customary in the regimented British society of the time, Jardine was asked to lead the dance with the wife of Sir Malcolm Hailey, the Governor of U.P. She was a wrinkled and eccentric Italian woman. Jardine immediately upset protocol by leading off with the prettiest girl on the floor despite mild protests by Father, who was Deputy Commissioner at the time. But I suspect that Father was rather pleased, for Hailey had engineered his ouster from Balrampur not so long ago!

I first heard of the North Kheri forests when I discovered that Vizzy had taken Jardine there for a shoot. They stayed at a forest rest house called Chhanga Nala and slaughtered five tigers in as many days. Vizzy was connected to the rulers of Singahi, a local State which arranged shoots for British officials, and claimed that Kunwar Dilipat Shah, the uncle of the Raja, was the finest running game shot in the world, though how that classification was determined is a mystery. Vizzy's connection with Singahi was through his wife, who was the sister of the Raja of Kashipur, whose wife in turn was the daughter of the Commander-in-Chief of the Nepal army. The ruler of Singahi himself came from Nepal, from where he was pushed out, and had established himself by dispossessing one of the local rulers. Vizzy is supposed to have killed 383 tigers, but died as a result of an injured kidney when he fell off an elephant charged by a wounded tigress in a sugarcane field close to the State capital.

I did my Senior Cambridge examination in 1934, which was the height of my scholastic achievements. Despite my attempts at playing hooky, under my mother's vigilance I came first in my class. Compared to a previous year when the incumbent had come first in the British Empire, this was no great shakes, but it gave me the chance to make out that I had come first in the school, just like Harishwar Dayal.

Father was now transferred as Deputy Commissioner to Saharanpur, and I went to the Lucknow Christian College. I was supposed to stay with Ted Mumby, a fine athlete and a P.T. instructor from an American college; but he was on furlough and I stayed with the Raja of Mahmudabad, whose father had been a friend of my grandfather. While in school, and persuaded by my sickly childhood and lack of prowess at games, I had started weight training. Charles Atlas and his Dynamic Tension were supposed to help one build lissom musculature, and Atlas' handsome face was the rage. Without the guidance I had in school, I started staying away from college classes in the interests of building bigger biceps.

Ted Mumby returned from the United States and I took up a course in wrestling under his instruction, but was refused permission by my parents to attend a wrestling Meet. They realized that I was neglecting my studies. I wasted my leisure hours, which were plenty, and faithful old Tanna from the Kumaun hills, who looked after me, complained to my parents that I was wasting my time. I was invited one night to attend a champagne reception for the Viceroy and got so inebriated that I had difficulty in finding my way back to Mahmudabad House, though it was hardly a hundred yards away. When I woke the faithful Tanna, he was disgusted to find that I had been sick in my pockets in some unaccountable way. I sat for the Intermediate examination, for which I was unprepared, and then went to Uncle Shummy and Aunty B in Simla. There I scanned the result sheet in the newspaper for a long time before making the inane statement that my name was not in it. Father and Mother were in Simla at the time, and mercifully took the news of my failure with great tolerance.

Jumper in the mean time had been doing well at the Indian Military Academy, the training centre which had taken the place of Sandhurst for officers of the Indian Army. He did not do well initially, but his Company Commander, a Major Frank Moore, recognizing hidden potential, promoted him to the rank of Lance Corporal during his first term. The allocation of responsibility paid off, and Jumper became one of the outstanding cadets of the Academy. He won four Blues in games, and at the end of his final term after two and a half years, he was a colour sergeant at the annual passing out parade. He was a talented actor and mimic, had a good singing voice, generally was a most attractive and well-liked personality, and very popular with the opposite sex. His natural attainments did not require him to prove himself through the destruction of trophy animals.

Saharanpur was within a short driving distance of Dehra Dun, and I would accompany my parents to watch ceremonial parades, and other sporting functions, including cycle polo, at the Academy, where Jaswant was one of the smartest cadets. In between the two cities lay extensive forested areas, where we would go for Christmas shoots. Some of Jaswant's instructors were invited, among them a Captain Kirkwood who nearly shot me when he aimed at a sambhar which crossed the line, and on whose daughter Doreen my brother was very keen, and with whom he acted in plays. They sang the duets of 'Rosemarie' and the 'Indian Love Call' together. There was also John Martyn, Balram's House Master at Doon School, and Pansy Wood, the Superintendent of Police at Saharanpur, with his London-born wife who taught us to sing bawdy songs. These we sang with great gusto before the campfire, as well as old-time favourite like 'Danny Boy', and 'Annie Lawrie'. Teddy Hunt, Pansy's successor, sought to take his place by the logfire, and sang a most dreary song in a tuneless voice about legal tender which he termed 'Spindukliums'. He claimed this had been sung by Freddy Young, the policeman who had captured Sultana, a celebrated dacoit, by the simple process of falling on him. Freddy weighed 280 pounds.

We were supposed to shoot jungle fowl for the pot, but were so inept at this that the camp was soon subsisting on a vegetarian diet, and Father had to take a hand, or rather a gun, in remedying our plight—something he had forsworn in Balrampur. Uncle Dalip distinguished himself by firing at a swarm of bees—their vast numbers were not much affected by the pellets, but they were irritated and stung the other shooters. Aunt B shot a pig, the only animal she had ever killed, as she was a non-violent disciple of Gandhi. Uncle Shummy saw a hyena I had wounded in the hind quarters, and thought that all hyenas had red tails. I sat with him on a machan in a tiger beat, but he got cramps and I had to get off the machan to fetch some article he had left at the foot of the tree. A young tiger appeared and passed by; Jumper fired and wounded the animal. Father and I went after the wounded tiger, one of the most dangerous animals. We had to climb a hill, which is one of the most risky ways of tracking a wounded tiger, as it should be approached if possible down hill. Fortunately, the tiger had been shot through the liver and its hindquarters were paralysed; it was only able to lift its head and snarl. Father was in the lead, but I was alarmed to note that his weapon was shaking after the stiff climb, when I stepped in front and gave the animal the quietus.

Jaswant soon passed out of the Military Academy and was posted for a year's attachment to the Royal Fusiliers, a British regiment, where he was enormously popular. He trained their hockey team and was known as a pocket Hercules, for he was short in stature. He was immensely strong, and we took part in a wrestling meet at the Rink in Mussoorie when he came on leave. Though keener on other sporting events, Jaswant, inspired by his intense competitive spirit, won his bout, whereas I, who went in with a hearsay reputation, suffered ignominious defeat. After his attachment he was posted to the 4/12 Frontier Force Regiment, and saw action at Fort Jamrud against the Pathans, who also provided most of the soldiers in his own regiment. On coming on leave, Jaswant brought with him up to the Savoy Hotel in Mussoorie a Walter Fisher from his regiment. We had a wonderful time, but I was ultimately sent off to Lucknow because, in euphoric competition with earning lieutenants, I had exceeded my allowance. Jaswant was presented with a car on his passing out of the Academy, and such was his *joie de vivre* that he wrenched the steering wheel off its stand on a sharp turning and nearly ran off the Attòck Bridge and into the river.

Jaswant went on to Lahore and beat a Captain Clynton Reed to win the Army Tennis Championship, which he held for two years. He also got very close to beating D.N. Capoor, then ranked No. 2 in India, at the U.P. Championship at Oudh Gymkhana Club. Stories kept seeping back of his wild ways through the faithful Tanna, now with Jaswant; Tanna observed that, though Jaswant was popular with women, his friend Niranjan Prasad used to entice them away, but by what means he did not specify. When Tanna remonstrated at the wild ways of these young men, he claimed that they chased him in the small hours trying to empty their swollen bladders on him. However, soon war clouds started gathering and both Jaswant and Niranjan Prasad were seconded to the Indian Air Force.

Balram, possibly the most talented of us brothers, passed out of Doon School. Its founder Principal, A.E. Foote, had been Headmaster at Eton; John Martyn was a former master at Harrow, and there were other teachers who were distinguished in both scholastic and athletic pursuits. Balram signed the school honours book eleven times, and went on to a B.A. Honours at St Stephen's College in Delhi. When World War II broke out, Balram tried to enlist in the air force. He was sponsored by Micky Nethersole, D.S.O., Croix De Guerre, who was in the I.C.S. and an air ace of the First War in the company of Macudden and Ball, both V.Cs. Micky used to relate that his greatest act of bravery was when the French Commander-in-Chief pinned the Cross of War to his flesh as well as his tunic, and he did not flinch! Balram was the same height as Jaswant, but the effort to get him into the air force had been so publicized that it became impossible for the recruiting authorities to resile from the pronouncement that his legs were shorter than that required in a pilot. He thus ended up as a Calcutta boxwallah.

Meanwhile, I barely passed my Intermediate from Meerut, and then went on to Allahabad University. Here, too, I exercised, wrestled and continued weightlifting. I wrestled with an enormous Sikh who lay on me and I could not move. I joined the University Training Corps, and was bayonetted by my neighbour while indulging in bayonet practise. I passed my B.A. and sat the Indian Police examination. By then war had broken out and I threw out my text books. My parents had promised to send me to Oxford if I did well in my B.A., but going abroad at this juncture was not possible; in any case, my academic performance had been undistinguished.

A brief account of the activities of my elder brother runs through this narrative because I have attempted to show that the desire to kill compulsively is not an atavistic inheritance, but a deep complex of redirected aggression triggered by an insufficiency in the so-called sport hunter. In my own example, I see that a sickly childhood and a natural denial of talent led me to try proving myself in society. My brother, with his inborn abilities, was able to achieve competitive excellence unassisted. In contrast, I, whose development was retarded by sickness, had to rely on medical treatment, on physical exercise, and on sophisticated weaponry to overcome the powerful presence of animals as symbols of achievement. In every 'sport hunter', there probably lies an imbalance which he feels must be evened out in the society to which he belongs by the destruction of a symbol.

After I passed my examination at Allahabad University I had to think of getting a job, especially as any future plan of going to a foreign university had been upset. With my scholastic record, the Indian Civil Service was probably too stiff a competitive exam for me and I applied for the Indian Police. However, I botched my interview by expressing ignorance of the Polish Corridor, which was the burning event of the day, and I was innocent of any knowledge about an obscure dispute in Kanpur about Indian Christians. Thus, when Germany marched into Poland, and war was declared on 3 September 1939, I applied to join the army, and was accepted as an officer for a wartime commission. I was sent to the Indian Military Academy in Dehra Dun for a five-month crash course, a course it had taken my brother two and a half years to complete.

I arrived at the Academy in February 1940, and was posted to 'B' Company, to which by a coincidence Jaswant had also belonged. By a further coincidence, I was allotted the same orderly, whose main job was to bring me a cup of tea in the morning, and see that I went on parade in time, all spick and span, after which I was on my own. He was a particularly hard-bitten and organized character and, having been in service since the Academy was inaugurated, he knew many cadets and officers, both distinguished and undistinguished, who had

passed out under his basic impetus. He was so regimented in the performance of his job that my ordinarily lazy temperament was never
an excuse for being late. However, he had the embarrassing habit of
sprucing the sartorial appearance of his charge by darting his large
and horny hand under my khaki shorts to give the shirt tails a vicious
tug in order to smooth out the creases. His convulsive and indiscriminate grasp was agonizing on occasions, and I wondered whether
Jaswant had borne such torture with greater fortitude for two and a
half years.

Ragging by the senior cadets was de jure but, unlike in some
institutions, was undertaken with discretion, as befitted men about to
go forth into the world as officers and gentlemen. It was used
principally to prevent incoming cadets from arriving with superior
notions. One A.I.S. Dara arrived with his Olympic Gold Medal at
hockey prominently displayed. It was immediately consigned up his
rectum. I was let off because of my brother's record. Looking back, I
think I would have been better for being ragged.

While in Lucknow, before I joined the Academy, Father had met a
Brigadier of the Royal Artillery, who was so impressed by him that he
later asked for me to be posted to an artillery unit. So after my
crowded five-month course in Dehra Dun I took off to do a Gunner
Course at Kakul, which is just off Abbottabad, now in Pakistan, and
where the School of Artillery was before Partition. I had to change
trains at Lahore in order to get to Havelian, and from there by taxi to
reach Kakul. At Lahore station I met Jaswant, who was there on some
errand for the Air Force. He had his latest girlfriend with him, a nurse
who had at one time been in a hospital in Sri Lanka. We went to a
dance at Standard Restaurant in the evening and ran into Minu, with
his girlfriend, a young lady doctor. We thought we would form one
party, but when the two ladies confronted each other it was discovered that they had both been in the same hospital in Sri Lanka,
and were not on speaking terms. I had therefore to divide my time
between two tables, and enticing a cabaret artiste called Larissa from
her young Air Force chaperone, a task in which I was unfortunately
unsuccessful.

The next day I continued my journey to Kakul, where I found the
technicalities of gunnery of extraordinary interest, and the operation
of big guns more appealing than the square bashing of the infantry,
though it was said that the infantry was the queen of the battlefield.
Tucked away in the mountains, Kakul was an ideal station for gunnery practice, and it gave one a sense of extraordinary ability to direct
the fire power of the great howitzers on to the opposite slopes, and

see the shell craters formed by the flying detritus of quartz, shrapnel discharging its deathly spray, or to watch colourful tracer bullets zeroing on to their tank targets. We played hockey and football against neighbouring units, had parties in the Mess, and generally the relationship with our instructors was relaxed compared to that with drill sergeants who delighted in awarding us extra drills or 'Puttie Parades' at the Academy.

After an attachment with a Royal Artillery regiment, regular officers passed out at the end of a ten-week course at Kakul, but officer cadets from the Academy did an extra course and it was not till 28 December 1940 that I was posted to the 'A' Field Regiment at Deolali. This was the first Indian artillery field regiment and was horse-drawn; except for the Commanding Officer, and Battery Commanders, it consisted entirely of Indian commissioned officers. There was an assortment of junior officers, including Mark Ranganathan. He had won both the Sword of Honour and the Gold Medal at the IMA, and four Blues in team games. A brilliant young officer with enormous potential, everything came too easily to him, and he was cashiered for over indulgence in drink. On the other end of the line, there was Gurdev Singh who was so inept a horseman that he created a Guiness record on a ceremonial occasion by climbing up a horse from one side and falling off the other.

After some months of regimental duty I was sent for a PT course to Kasauli. Before leaving, I was told by my Troop Commander that I would be allowed to go on leave. However, after I finished the course I had still not heard of my leave, so instead of reporting back I sent a telegram to the Troop Commander, Bertie Litchfield, that I was going on leave according to my conversation with him. I received a peremptory telegram from Donald Adams who had taken over the Third Battery from an old fuddy duddy, Bill Barlow, a First War veteran.

I hurried back and was greeted by a rocket from Adams. Unfortunately, and wrongly, I felt mistreated and sought the advice of an ICS officer who had been seconded to the Regiment. He made out that this was an anti-Indian move and advised me to send an application to my erstwhile sponsor, Brigadier Dennis, who was the Commander, Royal Artillery of the 17th Division. Dennis was disgusted with me to say the least, and the heat was really on when it was recommended that I be put on Adverse Report after I had applied for a transfer to Mountain Artillery. Donald Adams made out that I was afraid of going on active service by applying as a second choice for a posting to the Artillery Training Centre. Efforts were now made to patch up the whole affair, but events had gone too far, and as the First Field Regiment was due to go to Burma with the 17th Indian Division, and as Officers on Adverse Report were not allowed to go on active service, I was sent to the Second Indian Anti-Tank Regiment in Hyderabad, Sind. After a few months they also went off on active service, and I was once again shuttled around, this time to the Fifth Maratha Anti-Tank Regiment.

It was with this unit that I went overseas, for my Adverse Report had by now run out. We were sent to join the Tenth Indian Army, as a part of what was known as the PAI (Persia and Iraq) Force, consisting mostly of second echelon troops, as the fighting formations were lined up in the Middle East against the Afrika Korp. The fifth Anti-Tank were stationed at Babina in Jhansi, and I went to Lucknow to say farewell. Father had been promoted as Secretary to the U.P. government in the Information Department, and decorated with the award of a C.I.E. for his services in settling the Shia-Sunni dispute as Deputy Commissioner, Lucknow, of which post he was the first Indian incumbent. As we parted at the station, he said, 'Do your best. I know you will never falter or fail'. He looked reassuring and indestructible as the train steamed out, but I did not know that I would never see him again.

We sailed for Iraq from Bombay and landed at Basra, and en-camped at Zubair about twelve miles from the Shatt-el-Arab, the junction of the Euphrates and the Tigris. The unending feature of sand was dreary and depressing, and the heat and sandy grit which penetrated every crevice made us wonder why we were fighting for such a portion of the globe. As one British Other Rank wrote to his family, 'I am not allowed to say where we are, but I am at the arsehole of the world and gradually travelling up it.' The censor considered that he did not need to use his scissors. We dug bore holes as latrines and, when they were full, just moved on. Distances were limitless. After a few months we moved to Musaiyab outside Baghdad, where the atmosphere was more congenial, and we could sample the fleshpots on occasions. One night we found ourself in the redlight area with a wide assortment of residential inmates. There was a Chinese incumbent and, while we were disputing whether a certain reputed peculiarity among Chinese women was genuine, and one of our company had denied the allegation, we were nabbed by the Military Police and duly appeared before our Commanding Officer, who curtailed everyone's leave.

While the Alamein flap was on we received hurried instructions to proceed as reinforcements to the Western desert, but this was soon cancelled when it was discovered that we were armed with World War I eighteen-pounder guns and had to borrow transport from the local Service Corps to take our guns from A to B.

During our stay outside Baghdad I received a telegram from Jaswant to say that father had died suddenly of typhoid. I went to my tent and wept inconsolably. It was just not possible. I took out a bottle of whisky and attempted to drink myself into a stupor, but was violently sick. I got leave from the Commanding Officer, and arrived in Lucknow to find my mother, brothers and sister overwhelmed by the tragedy which had overcome us. Apparently he had been recovering and there was talk of his going on leave when he had a relapse. The fact that a few years later, with the discovery of antibiotics, typhoid has ceased to be a killer illness, is now in the realm of what might have been. Father had died intestate, while he still had seven years of service left. Mother had to get financial documents cleared, and look for a place to stay in. We rented a house, and later bought one of our own.

Jaswant had been at Cox's Bazar in Burma, commanding 2 Squadron of the Indian Air Force, where he had lead his Hurricanes in strafing the Japanese on Ramree Island. He related lurid tales of Mess parties with their Commanding Officer, Air Commodore the Earl of Bandon, popularly known as the Abandoned Earl, one of the wild band of Death or Glory Boys.

I had been granted a month's compassionate leave, but by the time I got back, having waited for ship accommodation, it was nearly two months. The C.O. accused me of conniving with the shipment authorities to spend Christmas at home, though initially the Shipping Officer would not believe I was a Christian.

On arrival I was told that the regiment was due to move up to Persia, to a place called Sultanabad, and then perhaps to Teheran, a prospect which excited us entertainment-starved junior officers no end. I accompanied the guns in a north-bound train from Basra, and it was a relief to get into the mountains, after the year we had spent in the monotonous vista of sand, heat and flies. Sultanabad was cold, and the deep pits we dug in the rocks under the shelter of our tents were more to keep out the chilly winds than against any surprise attack from dive bombers. I acquired an orderly who answered with equal alacrity to the pseudonym of Bloody Fool or Arsehole, but he was not as simple as he appeared, and I found that he was regularly siphoning money out of my purse. This I discovered only when he brought me one of my larger denomination notes, with an inquiry as to how much he could expect for it. I therefore had to return him to where he came from. So I suppose he was simple after all.

After a couple of months we heard that we were not earmarked for Teheran, but were returning to India. Once again I was detailed to accompany the guns, this time with an officer, Major Ball. We loaded the equipment onto a paddle steamer and sailed down the river Awaz, bound for our old base of Basra. This trip made up for the year of boredom which characterized our trip to the End of the World. We embarked at Awaz, passed Andemishk where the temperature was 137° F, and Kermanshah. The river was not wide, and the sides were lined with reeds growing with the riverain moisture. Beyond stretched the illimitable desert. Herds of small desert gazelle, somewhat like our own chinkara, congregated on the banks. Goli, as Ball was known, issued me with a rifle and as much ammunition as I wished, or used. The trip lasted ten days, and we lived like monarchs. No Reveille broke the dawn silence, and we got up when we wished. The day resounded to incessant rifle fire, and at night we drank whisky by moonlight, interrupting the proceedings now and again to let loose a fusillade at ghostly figures flitting in the moonlight. What we killed we picked up; the wounded were left. It was a disgusting exhibition of compulsive slaughter, and I now shudder at the memory of it. However, all things, good and evil, must end, and we came at last to Basra.

We were informed on the way that we had been attached to the famous Fourth Indian Division, and to refit and go on to Burma. We were proud that we were at last going into battle with a proven fighting unit. However, the odds, and our meagre understanding, were at fault and we were merely baggage carriers for the Division, and jettisoned as soon as we arrived in India. We were retained in Ranchi on garrison duties.

The time had now come to examine my standing vis-à-vis an army career. I had been commissioned as a rather underdeveloped officer and at a disadvantage with my peers. By a combination of fortuitous circumstance I had been posted to the select First Field Regiment, but thanks to my own wrong-headedness and unsolicited and wrong guidance, I had been branded unfit for active service, and been defeated in the purpose for which I had originally joined the army. When spanking new 25-pounders with their Spider Karrier four-wheel drive towing vehicles had arrived, and I had caught up with other officers and begun enjoying the performance of my duties after a slow start, I was sent away. However bitterly I regretted my thought-

less behaviour, there was little I could do and had to make the best
of it. I was sent to the Second Anti-Tank Regiment, but it, too, had to
leave me behind because army rules did not permit officers on special
reports to possibly endanger the functioning of a unit by going to war
with them.

I was then sent to a unit which had been converted from infantry
to anti-tank. Their inefficiency was accepted when they were issued
with out-of-date weaponry and directed to rely on other units for
transport. Their farcical existence was underlined when the Alamein
flap was on, but it was discovered that we had no transport to get the
guns to Egypt. We play-acted as toy soldiers, dug boreholes in the
sand, and returned to India acting as baggage carriers for a fighting
formation. I felt that my gunnery training had been wasted. I did not
get on with my Commanding Officer, nor did I care for the men I
served with, and what rankled was that the predicament was my fault.

I applied for a transfer to the Indian Air Force, or other civilian
occupation on the ostensible excuse of being superseded for promo-
tion; not surprisingly, I was put on an Adverse Report for the second
time. I was summoned for an interview at Delhi, and stopped over to
see Frank Moore, now a Major-General commanding 14 Division who
had employed Jim Corbett to train British soldiers in jungle warfare.
He talked with great affection of Jaswant, and how he had helped
him when he appeared to be losing direction. He wrote to Army
Headquarters offering to take me into his Division, but was told to
mind his own business. I was interviewed by the Military Secretary
and asked to resign or be cashiered. I had Faltered and Failed; and
my beloved father was not alive to take the rap.

3 From Killer to Conservation

The beauty and genius of a work of art may be reconceived, though its first material expression be destroyed. A vanished harmony may yet again inspire the composers, but when the last individual of a race of living beings breathes no more, another heaven and earth must pass before such a one can be again.

William Beebe (1877–1962)

THE War had ended, and many people were looking for ways of reordering their lives. Some were war heroes, others did not want to make the army a career, and some were dropouts. I tried to get a job with a couple of business firms, but nothing came of that.

It was now that destiny took a hand. Jaswant was eminently suited for a life in the armed forces, and he had found his niche. Balram should also have joined the Forces, but, thanks to some inopportune manoeuvrings to remove a somewhat meaningless hurdle to his recruitment into the air force, he had been compelled to join a business concern. In my case, circumstance, and the possible qualification of singlemindedness, or perhaps perversity of character, guided me from being a confirmed killer to become an ardent conservationist and a crusader for a lost cause.

If I had tried long enough I expect I would have landed a normal job. But I happened to meet Jai Singh, the younger brother of the Raja of Bijwa, a small feudal State near the Nepal border, who had just started farming on land leased from George Hearsey. He was a descendant of general Sir John Hersey who had tried quelling the 1857 mutiny in Barackpore by shooting Mangal Pandey. George was a pioneer farmer, and before the War had been using tractors, and also sowing soya beans, which was so in advance of the times that he was unable to find a market for them and went bankrupt as his warehouse filled with an unsaleable product. He called Palia 'the Chicago of the East', presumably because it was on a trade route from Nepal.

During the recently concluded war he had joined the army in some obscure administrative capacity, and, after demobilization, returned to resume farming. He had married a courtesan during the First War, but she had left him. This time he brought with him a young model from England, whom he had presumably inveigled into coming out to India inspired by the illusion of his vast acreage of rolling farmland. He tried to retain her affections by playing childish games, which involved hiding money and guiding her to find it! However, other predators were on the prowl, and an Anglo-Indian criminal lawyer named Walford was overheard by Hearsey making infamous proposals to her. Unfortunately, in his eagerness to eavesdrop, Hearsey fell over a flowerpot and, as Walford came out to investigate, he punched the latter on the nose, whereupon Walford instituted a case of trespass and assault. Younger aspirants were also lining up, and Jai, while paying nominal homage to his landlord Uncle George, was not averse to entertaining Hearsey's young wife. In the end, the lady found the situation too embarrassing to endure, and returned to the country of her origin, leaving a disillusioned Hearsey to his own devices.

In the mean time I was exploring the possibilities of farming as a career. I sought advice from a variety of people, and the consensus was that, as a farmer, you could not starve and that it was thus a worthwhile life. I went to stay with the Raja of Bijwa at Bhira, ten miles away from Palia, where he had a farm. We visited the Sarda river between Palia and Bhira and heard the hooves of swampdeer thundering as they galloped through the tamarisk which lined the banks. In the evening we sat over a kill by a tigress of a bullock, which had strayed into the forest. At night we drank whisky from a tooth-mug, and farming under such conditions seemed an enchanting prospect. I went to Palia and selected a plot of 750 acres as farmland, and when I was warned of the depredations of a myriad wild animals, who competed with human beings for their agricultural crops, I foresaw my role as the holder of a thin red line. I bought myself a ·275 bore Mauser rifle, and was ready to start my farming career.

I was on the passenger train from Lucknow, where my mother had now bought a house. The train drew into the Palia Kalan railway station at 3.30 in the morning of 1 May 1945. It was to go on to the Nepal border, a few stations ahead, which accounted for the extraordinary time of disembarkation. A small bullock cart known as a *lehru* was waiting for me and, as it a was moonlit night, I loaded my luggage on to it before setting off on the three-mile walk along the dirt track road which led to my farm site. Further north, another road known as the Prince of Wales Road ran a parallel course to the west, but it was now so overgrown with grass as to be unusable. Reputedly, this road had been made at some indefinite time when the Prince of Wales had come pigsticking to a place called Dhaka. The track was deeply rutted, and ankle deep in dust, but the stars shone brightly, and a waning moon lit the twin ribbons ahead. To the north, an Indian fox (*Vulpes Bengalensis*) gave a chattering bark, while in the copse a pack of jackals (*Canis Aureus*) sang their eerie falsetto chorus: 'Dead Hindu. Dead Hindu. Where are you? Where are you? Heree, Heeere.'

The sky was paling as I approached Jasbirnagar, which was what I had decided to call my farm, and further on a hogdeer (*Axis Porcinus*) fled with consecutive piping whistles of alarm. The sawing grunts of a leopard as it retired to its lair indicated what had frightened the deer. As I turned into my land, a vista of grassland stretched endlessly to the west. A herd of twenty Nilgai, India's large antelope (*Boselaphus Tragocamelus*) stood in an opening. The burly, slaty grey bulls with their sloping withers, contrasting with the more numerous, beige coloured females with their white stockings, and further on, a large herd of black buck (*Antelope Cervicapra*) cropped the short Imperata grass. The heads of numerous cattle, both cows and buffaloes, glinted in the light of the dawn. In front of me lay most of what I would have to contend with if I was going to make a success of farming.

As I had no place to live in I made my temporary headquarters at Jai Singh's, which also happened to be close to the village of Maraucha, where most of the cattle were owned by Gaddis, Muslim graziers. I got hold of some labourers to build me a grass hut, but as I had heard that the workmen were very slack, I stood over them, supervising their labour in the heat of the day, and went down with a bad attack of heatstroke.

On recovery, I bought some buffaloes and ploughshares to break the land and sow paddy as a monsoon crop. All the money I had was from my slender savings in the army, and I soon started running out of funds. However, my troubles were only starting, and they soon lined up in formidable proportions! Soon after the crop was sown, the young shoots were grazed by the numerous ungulates who had hitherto held undisputed sway over the area. The wild animals could be chased away, but the livestock was not so easily manageable. Moreover, the Gaddis resented my arrival to contest their right to indiscriminate grazing, though on the positive side they found their milch cattle were better nourished on succulent crops, and started to make a habit of releasing their unmanageable livestock to graze my agricultural crops.

I was soon embroiled in litigation with them. One day I found two bullocks grazing my fields. As they were very wild I was unable to catch and send them to the local cattle pound. I lamed one with a ·22 rifle, and subsequently caught and tethered the cattle, but foolishly gave the sorrowing owner a note to the local veterinarian to say that, as I could not catch these animals, I had been compelled to lame them, and would he treat them? The owner promptly went to court, and I was summoned before a magistrate at Lakhimpur, fifty-five miles away. After sundry negotiations, the matter was settled out of court, and I bought over the lamed animals. I subsequently sold them for more than I paid, and therefore won the first round. Numerous other cases were instituted, but by a mixture of cajolery and strong-arm tactics I held my own, and gradually the cattle owners realized that agriculture had come to stay, and soon the Gaddis themselves turned their efforts to farming.

Wild ungulates were more controllable and shy and, unlike the voracious cattle, had smaller appetites, and would therefore graze on the move. But, when the paddy grain began to ripen a new menace appeared in the shape of wild pigs. They would devastate overnight a crop ready to be harvested, and to approach a field at night was like a gala occasion at a Latin night club, as the champing of the ripe grain sounded like so many castanets. I built myself a portable machan, which I used to set up in the middle of a field and where I spent the night. I brought out an old ·500 Express which I had acquired before the War, and tried to shoot a record among the big, old boars. The biggest I could kill was one weighing 300 pounds, with tushes of eight inches, and I doubt if boars go a great deal beyond these dimensions.

As my farming activities increased, the competition from wild pigs became more acute. Sugarcane was their perennial delight, and they began their act as soon as it was sown. They would dig up the sets which were planted and covered with earth. After the sets had germinated they took shelter in the crop itself, and, as the cane matured, they would make shelters against rain and inclement weather by piling cane leaves in extensive heaps; getting under the pile of trash, they would elevate it to form a kind of igloo. They dug into the fresh earth to form breeding shelters, and bred outrageously large families, as is the wont amongst their kind. They lived in their larder, and ate at all hours. Their tribe grew in geometrical progression and increasingly competed with human beings for livelihood.

I employed a man as night watchman from the Pasi tribe. He was called Ram Dayal, but known as Dakua as he was an inveterate dacoit, and had been jailed a number of times. He was inordinately lazy and work shy, as behoves a man of his occupation who lives on the earned wealth of others, and the only recommendation which I found valid was that, as there was honour among thieves, no other miscreants would trespass on his preserve when he was ensconced. I found him quite amenable, apart from his obvious shortcomings. I gave him a thrashing periodically, which put the fear of god into him, and perhaps accounted for my immunity from larcenous activities.

One morning I was taken to where Ram Dayal was writhing in pain, presumably back from some thieving expedition, and was told that he had been bitten by a snake. I saw twin fang marks on his toe. It is known that a large number of snake-bites and deaths are caused by shock, under the presumption that all snakes are poisonous, but I felt this was the real McCoy. I tied a ligature above the wound, cut into the two fang marks with a razor blade, and sucked Ram Dayal's grimy toe. I sent him to the doctor who gave him some sort of injection, and he was well the following day. This act of mine may also have inspired a certain loyalty, for though he had the chance, he never stole anything of mine, and when he did disappear, unable to stand the strain of manual labour, he contented himself with removing my manager's watch and a few other sundry articles.

While Dakua had been with me he introduced me to other members of his tribe, as they specialized in netting pigs. The nets consisted of woven mesh made of stout rope, each net being the width of a tennis court. They were then stood up supported by unconnected stakes on the ground at right angles to the line along which the pigs were being driven, and behind cover. As the pigs rushed off, they got entangled in the nets which collapsed upon them as the stakes fell away. The pigs were then killed by belabouring with cudgels. It was said by these stalwarts that it took a whole night's belabouring to kill a big pig. The screams of agony, of course, were horrendous. I employed these professionals sometimes, and occasionally a tiger got caught. However, these animals were too powerful and heavily armed, and bit their way out of the mesh, while no human dared to come close, and their deafening roars on a dark night were forbidding sounds. Soon I came to terms with such adversities, and learned to live with them.

Gradually, I found that breaking up the land with animal power was an exacting process and, with help of Micky Nethersole, who was then what was known as the Senior Member, Board of Revenue, I took a loan from the government and bought a tractor. Unfortunately, the tractor was a small three-wheeler called a John Deere Model 'B', and not sufficiently powerful to control even a fraction of the 750 acres in my possession. By unfortunate hindsight I kept on discovering that, as in business, one should not under-power or under-finance in agriculture, though people are inclined to believe that farming is a poor man's enterprise and can be built up on a shoe string. However, even with my small tractor, which I drove myself, I found life was much easier. Micky Nethersole departed with Indian Independence in 1947, so further help from the government as a source of finance dried up. Also, I found that repayment under strict government regulations was rather more unpleasant than drawing a cheque on the Treasury. I therefore took a loan from a bank on the security of family investments.

Hitherto I had spent most of my time consolidating my venture into farming, but now, as crops started yielding a small income, I found time to look around. The North Kheri Forest Division was a commercial, working forest where a number of valuable timber trees were auctioned to private contractors by the Forest Department. Also, the Division was divided into a number of shooting blocks, which could be applied for on a roster basis, and where we were allowed to shoot a specified number of animals and live in one of the forest rest houses. I tried to get a shooting block every Christmas; this was more in the shape of a family and friends re-union rather than a serious shoot, though the old urge for slaughter was still smouldering and the destruction of the master predator dominated all desires.

My elder brother came from whichever air force station he was posted at, and would arrive in solitary splendour, much to everyone's amusement, whereas his wife, who was the daughter of the then Chief Minister of the North-West Frontier Province, would arrive the next day with the children and heavy luggage. Mariam was that ideal product, according to Kipling, of the marriage between a Pathan father and a Scots mother, with the virility of the one and the dourness and canniness of the other. Her marriage was the cause of a political upheaval as her father's political opponents made out that it was an out-of-caste union between a Sikh and a Muslim, though Jaswant was shaven and shorn and baptised a Christian, a kindred 'people of the book'. Mariam's heavily burdened arrival was accorded an extreme welcome, as she was very popular with all of us, and Jaswant was ribbed for shedding all responsibility while his wife bore the entire burden of travel.

Though Jaswant was the eldest of the family, he probably enjoyed himself the most, possibly because he was able to relax the iron discipline he normally imposed upon himself, which made him the most feared of senior officers on parade, and the most loved during leisure hours. He would appear in the early morning unshaven and unkempt, in an old balaclava to keep out the chill, and which we claimed he had pilfered from an ancient mechanic engaged in boring a tube well, and known as the 'Boring Babu.' He took great delight in identifying himself with the staff, and would drive the John Deere 'B', which towed the generator into camp. When the tractor broke down or got bogged, Jaswant would insist on going without his meals to keep the staff company, reminding one of the inscription in Chetwode Hall of the Indian Military Academy: 'The safety, honour and welfare of your country comes first, always and every time. The honour, welfare and comfort of the men you command come next. Your own ease, comfort and safety come last, always and every time.' Balram also arrived with convivial bachelor friends from Calcutta, and my sister Amar, who had married in London, sometimes came with her two children.

Our first Christmas was a modest affair, as the elephant which I had arranged to borrow never arrived, and the car which I tried to arrange developed engine trouble; but later, when I had acquired both forms of conveyance, the move out to Christmas camp was more elaborate. With Jaswant's help I bought a generator which had been used to light air force stations during the War, and the celebration of Christmas became a complex affair. Unlike deadly hunters who objected to the sound of the generating engine which disturbed wild animals, the noise and light added to the gaiety of the log fire, and the songs of earlier days were sung. It was Balrampur all over again, except that the *dramatis personae* was different.

One Christmas John Withnell, who shared a 'chummery' with Balram in Calcutta, arrived. He was a fine sportsman and rugger player, and one day we went to a marshy lake called Bhadi Tal. There we shot a couple of swampdeer, but on return were informed by the forest guard that it was a protected species and he would have to report the matter to his superior officer. In reality he was angling for a payoff, but we pre-empted his intentions by reporting our error to the Divisional Forest Officer, and got away with a good word for our honesty in confessing the mistake.

Later in the lake area we came upon a young chital fawn crouched in its form. As it got up to run, John made a fine flying tackle and grabbed the young animal by its leg. I unimaginatively named it Bambi, and brought it back to the farm at Jasbirnagar. It turned out to be a male and became so tame that it would follow me with my dogs, feed with them and even lick the milk from their jowls after they had emptied their saucers clean. Bambi was very gentle until, as a yearling, he came into hard horn, which is the timing of the rut, and the period during which deer get aggressive with their own species in the wilds. Soon I was accosted by a neighbour who complained that, when trying to drive the chital out of his paddy field he was grazing, Bambi, with his lack of female companions or male competitors and used to the human presence, had gored him. But his horns though sharp were small, and I was able to persuade the complainant that such an incident would not recur.

However, the following year as a brocket he assumed a more formidable presence, and though very affectionate with me—he slept near my bed—he took a violent aversion to my cook. One evening while dozing near the camp fire my subconscious registered a yelling, which seemed to be coming closer. It was the cook, who had abandoned my dinner and taken flight, pursued by Bambi. He was knocked down with rescue in sight, and would doubtless have suffered severe injury had I not leapt up and grabbed the chital by his horns. Blind with rage he went for me, and as we wrestled in the glow of the log fire his brow tine split my bicep, which scar I still carry forty years later. However, I was still the stronger and Bambi soon called enough.

The cook resumed his cooking of dinner, and Bambi, as if nothing had happened, came to his usual resting place at the side of my bed. Next morning we knocked him down and castrated him. Unused to such rough treatment he disappeared for two days, and just as I was mourning his loss, he arrived back on the third day and resumed life from where he had left off. The next, and third year, he grew a fine pair of antlers, but they never came into hard horn, presumably because of the castration. One morning he simply disappeared, and I searched everywhere for him. I thought that a predator might have got him, but then a few days later I saw him running away. I called to him, and he stopped, looked at me in recognition, and resumed his flight. I never saw him again, and hope that he met others of his kind, and was accepted by them. Years later, I tried to reintroduce a young female to a local herd and she had been rejected. As in the lion pride, apart from males, herds are perhaps based on familial extraction.

I kept other pets, both chital and hogdeer, but they were all eventually killed by wayfarers on the look-out for easy meat. Cymbeline used to share his roti with an elephant, but one day when I found him with his legs broken by gypsies, and mangled by killer dogs, I decided that as a human I had no right to take an animal from its environment for my pleasure. I had tethered an eighteen-foot python, but he too developed a sore on his back and died.

In the early 1950's the system of feudal rulers was abolished, and the State of Balrampur, faced with the imperative need of getting rid of its stable of elephants, had to decide what to do with them. My old guru, Lala Babu, had gone to the happy hunting grounds, and Butterfield had also passed on. I never discovered what happened to the great tuskers, Macdonald Bahadur and Kanhaiya, and presumably the skeleton of Chand Murat still collects grime in some government museum.

I had as my manager on the farm a man with whom I had played football in our youth, and one day I received a message through him that the State would like to present me with an elephant called Mabel Mala, who was supposedly named after my mother. However, I was informed that the elephant offered to me was getting on in age, and I would do better to get another one in her place. Thus, after sundry negotiations, Bhagwan Piari ('the Beloved of God') arrived with her *Filwan*, and Jafar the *Fil Tabib* (elephant doctor) who had been the *Filwan* of Kanhaiya when I was a boy in Balrampur. Bhagwan Piari, a fine looking elephant, about nine feet tall, was reputed to be about forty-five years old.

During my days at University I had taken to weight training, as already noted. This activity had, of course, been interrupted over the war years, but when I settled down to my new vocation I took up the weights once more. The American weightlifting Olympic team paid a visit to Calcutta and I went to see them. Together with the Russian team, they were the leading performers in this form of heavy athletics, and there was much competition between them. There was also a Mr Universe contest of bodybuilders, which the Russians scorned as they claimed that they would rather be strong men than earn plaudits by posing with a rose between their teeth! Secretly I agreed with the Russians, and over the years they became the leading nation at this form of athletics.

The American team had many world champions. Paul Anderson the heavyweight, Tommy Kono, middleweight, Pete George a lightweight champion at the age of seventeen, and Chuck Vinci, a diminutive bantam who lifted over twice his body weight. I was fascinated by the ease with which these athletes handled enormous weights, and bought myself an Olympic barbell. However, I had started too late, and, moreover, had to train alone. I went to Calcutta to train at the Muslim Institute, and got to lift 220 pounds in the Clean and Press, which was close to the record in my weight in India. But sadly, I performed this feat only once!

I tried to visit Calcutta more often as, apart from being able to work out with other weightlifting enthusiasts, Jaswant was posted there as Air Officer in Chief, commanding Eastern Air Command. Balram was also there in a business house. We spent the Christmas of 1962 together, and the Chinese invasion had just taken place. Jaswant had been under tremendous strain flying unpressurized aircraft at great altitudes, and was in fine form, as was natural in the aftermath of the ending of hostilities. His achievements in the war were considerable. Whereas his class-mates from the Military Academy, who were supposedly commanding fighting formations of the army in the inhospitable mountains, had fled abandoning their ill-equipped troops, Jaswant had proved an example to his Command. He was decorated in 'the performance of a task beyond the normal course of duty.' We saw the New Year in to the nostalgic tune of 'Auld Lang Syne', but that was his farewell, for he had a fatal heart attack. Those the gods love die young. We were devastated, for he was only forty-seven years old. Calcutta, the dirtiest and friendliest city in India, now lost all its charm for me.

Some time later, Mohammed Ali, after his retirement, visited India. His three fights with Joe Frazier were in the legend book, and the 'Thriller in Manila' was the ultimate in punishment that one man could take from another. Ali had regained his crown in a fabulous fight with George Foreman at Kinshasa, and had retired disproving the theory that they never come back. He once came into the ring in Delhi, handsome and unmarked, with Jimmy Ellis for an exhibition bout. But a ring of fat showed round his midriff. Hawa Singh the Indian Heavyweight champion was given the honour of going into the ring with the Greatest and Prettiest of all time. He tried his utmost to land a telling punch, but as the round was closing Ali laid his hand on Hawa Singh's topknot and shook it as if to say, 'Well tried, Sonny'.

But for those whose meal ticket Ali was, he was immortal—the Legend that could never die, and they pulled him back again and again.

He was thrashed by his erstwhile sparring partner Larry Holmes, by Michael Spinks, and by fighters not fit to lace his boots. His features puffed and eyes dimmed, slurry of speech and mumbling platitudes, he now preaches the gospel of the Black Moslem.

Bhagwan Piari and I had many adventures during the twenty-five years that we were together, and I developed a great affection for her, and she for me, which she demonstrated by urinating copiously when I approached. While she was with me she eliminated a kidney stone weighing over half a kilogram, and narrowly escaped being crushed by a falling ficus tree during a thunderstorm. She attended all our Christmas camps, and I had my time cut out preventing her *Filwan*, Bhuntu, from purloining her Christmas rations to buy himself drink as he carried out parallel celebrations with his cronies. I often dismissed him for these misdemeanours; but he was good at his job, and I just as many times reinstated him. Eventually, smitten by asthma, his frail body wracked by indulgence in ganja and broken by an over-use of cheap alcohol, he abdicated in favour of his son. Bhuntu died shortly before Bhagwan Piari, and with their passing I too died a little.

Though elephants are nervous animals, Bhagwan Piari appeared unafraid of tigers, and I shot three so-called maneaters in her presence. She was present at the death of many more tigers, as well as assisting in the photography of others, and acquired a great reputation. April 1963 was a milestone in Bhagwan Piari's life. I had lent her to aid in the shikar of the Superintendent of Police, Kheri, who, unknown to me, passed her on to an industrialist from Kanpur. In early May she arrived at base with gaping fang marks on her left hind leg, where she had been mauled by a wounded tiger at Kiratpur about twenty miles north. Bhuntu considered this a suitable occasion for indulgence and, as I was supervising the medication of Bhagwan Piari's wounds, he related with elan that the tiger hunters, of whom there were many, had not bothered or dared to follow the ethic applied to the search for wounded animals, but had detailed subordinates to deal with the tiger. Bhuntu related with much bravado and probably little veracity that, when the wounded tiger charged the elephant, the mounted followers panicked, but that he had struck at the tiger with his Gajbag or ankus used to guide the elephant, and the tiger had then released his hold on Bhagwan Piari's leg, whereupon she had fled. A correspondence then ensued with the industrialist, from which I quote excerpts:

Every possible precaution was taken when attempting to recover the tiger. Nearly thirty dogs were used to trace it. On account of the dense foliage it took us two days to reach the brink of the nullah as we followed the blood which was found everywhere in gallons, with extreme caution.

On the third day, as was evident from his roars, the tiger could not climb the nullah, and when he did manage he could not move further and kept on roaring and roaring, when the elephant was asked to turn back. It was sheer bad luck that the tiger was lying somewhere under the dense foliage, and when the elephant came near he just attacked. From the above narration of facts it would be appreciated that it would not be fair to say that the tiger was wilfully abandoned, and that what was done was not against the ethics of good sportsmanship.

I am really surprised that you visited the nullah where the tiger was, the foliage was so dense and there were so many dry leaves, that the tiger would immediately detect the approach of anyone, and if alive would attack anything which comes near him. Anyway it is very nice of you to offer your cooperation.

The letter was in reply to one from me detailing my visits and accusing the industrialist of not following the wounded animal and, moreover, endangering my elephant which he had used without my permission. A second letter was more categorical, and elicited an acrimonious reply:

Thus the description of your valiant visits to the nullah, particularly the second when you once again searched it, where the tiger had been wounded, outwit even the story of Arabian Nights entertainment.

Similarly your claim to the ownership of the carnivora stocked in the forest which made you suggest 'To forego my annual campaign' against what you call our carnivora, outclasses the story of King Canute, who claimed rulership of the waves.

Similarly your ideas of inadequacy of firearms, and shikaris must be indeed amazing. If one Hollands ·465 D.B., two 450/400 D.Bs and two Hollands ·375 Magnum, carried by as many shikaris as the number of rifles, and a host of other rifles carried by Nepali residents are considered inadequate, then perhaps a battalion, armed with mortars and cannon would be necessary to track a tiger hit by two ·465 bore bullets.

You are at the fringe of libel when you say I can be charged with a heinous crime.

I wrote back to say: 'Your description of the armoury used against the tiger is impressive, but as you will agree, it is the man behind the gun that counts', . . . 'The Divine Conscience dwells in all of us, and though often obscured by self interest, and stunted by disuse, it does stand forth as a beacon for decent behaviour.' Correspondence then ceased, but I have given extracts in some detail because it illustrates the attitude of so-called sportsmen to the hunting of wild animals, the awe in which the tiger is held, and the animal's capacity for inflicting injury when aroused.

Subsequent events connected with this episode were as follows: a few days after the tiger was wounded, on 26 April 1963 the Range Officer, a forest guard and a number of Tharus from the village of Kiratpur, went to visit the place where the tiger had been hit, hoping it was dead; he charged out at the party. The portly Range Officer led the retreat, but the forest guard was mauled. Soon after the wounded Bhagwan Piari returned I took Bhuntu with me and went to the site where the tiger had been wounded. It was 10 May, and the tiger may just possibly have been alive as a kakar barked in the direction where the elephant had been mauled. The distance from Jasbirnagar was about thirty miles and we had started late. As it was turning into dusk, we came back from the mauling site. A week later we returned in the morning and, as we crossed the nullah, the rank smell of death assailed our senses. We came to a clearing which reminded me of a battlefield. Staves, shoes and clod hoppers littered the forest floor in profusion, and in the centre, as if still in authority, was the Range Officer's hat, and the bare bones of the tiger stripped of skin and flesh by scavengers, as he had evidently collapsed after his charge. I left the relicts where they belonged, and brought away one canine and a claw, and the Ranger's hat. I returned the hat to its owner and thought he looked somewhat sheepish. I have the canine as a souvenir, and was surprised to note that of its five inches as much as two-thirds were encased in the jawbone. The claw I gave to a woman friend, who has now disappeared with it, with my affection.

Bhagwan Piari's wounds healed slowly, as is the case with these pachyderms, but she now appeared to be more wary in the forest. Some time later I took her on a shoot in a nearby block. We were walking along a forest road when my companion turned and fired a shot in the undergrowth, and a tiger rushed away. He claimed that the tiger had been sitting sideways to us, but as we later discovered he had hit him low in the chest. We followed that tiger into dense grass, and suddenly he leapt on to the elephant next to mine and dug his claws into her head. Bhagwan Piari fled, and by the time she was brought under control, the man who had wounded the tiger and was on a third elephant, very commendably put a bullet into the enraged animal's brain. Bhagwan Piari, as so often happens with other elephants who are mauled, was now always nervous at the sight or smell of a tiger, and would not stand still when confronted, and fled many a time on later occasions. She died of old age when she fell into a shallow depression, and, with her head below the level of her body she was unable to get up. By the time we had dug enough to raise her head she was dead in the hot May sun. She was about seventy years old.

Though I was the original pioneer settler, other farmers started arriving towards the middle of the century. A large organization called 'The Collective Farms and Forests Ltd' started farming ten thousand acres. Other individuals followed suit as there was no restriction on the amount of land which could be leased. As crop damage by wild animals became distributed among other farmers, I bought two more, larger tractors to bring all my acreage under the plough.

But the landscape was changing. Whereas I had come to an endless vista of grassland, multi-coloured agricultural crops now shimmered on the horizon. Gone were the herds of Nilgai and blackbuck, and somehow the midnight cries of the fox and the jackal seemed muted. I conceived the idea of buying a crawler tractor to break up the land which was being settled by dispossessed personnel from Pakistan. Ahead lay extensive lands awaiting the plough: Majhra Singahi, the favourite hunting ground of Vizzy; and Khajuria, on the border of the districts of Pilibhit and Kheri—the haunt of robbers, of Kallan Khan who migrated to Pakistan and whose place was taken by Bashira, an ex-professional wrestler, and his gun-toting wife. Along the unending vista were grass hutments from where thin spirals of smoke snaked into the atmosphere. Some were the cooking fires of settlers who had arrived with the promise of large holdings. Others were funeral pyres for people from a dry temperature, enervated by recurrent malaria and the humid climate. Some gave their lives, but many stayed on, bolstered by the fact that they had nowhere else to go.

Once we camped at Mirchia Jheel, venue of the famous gubernatorial battues where forty trophy swampdeer stags would be gunned in a morning's shoot. Only a solitary female deer now splashed through the water, but further on a flight of mallard rose to the boom of a musket, leaving a couple lying in the water. On my return home I found that a neighbour of mine, one Boaz, had been raided by Bashira and his gun taken away. However, Boaz had been shooting tiger, so perhaps this was poetic justice. Another man named Agha, whose father had been with mine at Oxford, also took to shooting tigers on farmland, where there was no restriction on numbers. As his score grew, I suggested to the Chief Wildlife Warden that, as the end would justify the means, we should cook up a case against him. We did so, claiming that he had shot a tiger in the Reserved Forest. The Chief Wildlife Warden was unable to produce a witness, so I persuaded my tracker, who went by the name of Jackson, to give evidence. However, by threatening Jackson, the other side got him to refuse to falsify his statement, though I took him by the throat. But the case had a salutary effect, and Agha gave up his activities, alarmed by the notoriety, and migrated to Pakistan. Later, Bashira was gunned down in Pilibhit in an encounter with the police. His wife, the legendary gun-wielding Begum Bashira, turned out to be a non-descript and pregnant village woman; and the raid on my residence which was next on Bashira's list according to his diary, did not come about.

As though to underline that some wildlife was still left, two wolves raided my temporary premises at Jasbirnagar and took away a goat. I unashamedly shot one, but got no pleasure from this. The house that I was building was almost complete, but I felt no joy in occupying a building after over a decade of living in a straw hut. My feelings towards wildlife were at a stage of ambivalence, and killing no longer gave me a sense of achievement. I shot an old barasingha stag with antlers two inches off the world record given in Rowland Ward's book. The tamarisk brushwood lining the Sarda riverbed was being reclaimed by agriculturists, and no longer echoed to the pounding hooves of deer. Gaddis told me that barasinghas were still to be seen in large numbers in the area of Naudha Bhagar, a marshy river, where they took their cattle to graze every winter. I went there and saw remarkably large herds in segregated groups, their many tined antlers glittering in the morning sun. Land reclamation had already begun, and they were restless, and took off towards Ghola, an adjoining grassland of about three thousand acres with a lake in the centre.

On my return from this trip I determined to look for some land closer to the forest, for it seemed that overnight I had been smothered by cultivation. Khajuria and Majhra Singahi were also in the process of being reclaimed by a government colonization scheme to settle landless labour from eastern Uttar Pradesh. Government officials interpreted the colonization scheme in their own way, depending on the posts they were occupying, and would visit the colonization areas as a means of boosting their travelling allowances, as well as indulg-ing in forms of entertainment, chiefly shikar for which the area was famous, or smuggling from the Nepal border. One senior official had a tigress declared a maneater and it became known as the Maneater of Visenpuri; he shot an unidentified tigress and no doubt claimed a reward for killing the so-called maneater. The Commissioner of the neighbouring Nepal province of Dhangarhi was invited by his Indian counterpart to shoot a barasingha, though they were supposed to be protected in both countries. The Commissioner of Lucknow Division was brought a crocodile ensnared in a net which he was invited to shoot, and did so, believe it or not, from the safe distance of one metre.

I considered such incidents to be the lowest in depravity until I read in *Cat News 1991*, an official publication of the Species Survival Commission of the IUCN, the following nauseous extract: 'US Federal Officials are investigating more than a dozen ranches in the USA where "hunters" shoot tigers, jaguars, leopards and mountain lions. In some cases animals have been tranquillized and tied to trees and then shot, or released in areas the size of a football field to be killed by high-paying customers.'

A report in the *San Jose Mercury News* in California quoted Fish and Wildlife Service special agent Bill Talkin as saying one tiger at a Monterey Ranch was shot dead in its cage when it refused to move out. Witnesses said that another had walked less than thirty metres from its cage when it was shot. One of the ranchers charged, Floyd Lester Pearson III, told the newspaper that the 33 criminal charges against him were 'overblown'. 'The way they are talking about it like it was a crapshoot or something. It wasn't nothing like that. I am a hunter, and I lead guided hunts. There's nothing wrong with that!' Talkin said the Federal authorities confiscated photographs and videotapes of jaguars, tigers, leopards and mountain lions being shot on the Patterson property. The hunters came from all over the USA. The philosophy underlying such behaviour indicates a mental aberration.

Nepal was also changing direction. The King of Nepal shot a rhino in a Park to offer a blood libation to his ancestor. When I first arrived on the farm this Hindu kingdom was still in the thrall of the Middle Ages; with the King as the Divinity, the Ranas ruled the country, and its poverty was abysmal. Virulent malaria enervated the people, and wild animals competed with humans for existence. Sport hunting was the privilege of a few, and criminal punishment and procedures were primitive. The limited Rana rule had now gone. Everyone had Rights, and none Duties. The forests are going, and flash floods sweep down the great waterways. The Churia Range, traditional holding grounds of the tiger, is no more, and the harvest has been gleaned in India. The forests of Nepal, contiguous to the Dudhwa National Park, have been reclaimed for agriculture by ex-army personnel. Their cattle graze in our forests, and their fire arms decimate our wildlife. Buffer areas which were once pitted by tiger pugs and ungulate slots now only show signs of human occupation.

I had heard of land in an area known as Bilahia, which adjoined the Dudhwa Reserved Forest and which had been leased by a politician whose original plan was to use his location next to the forest to extract timber. He had indeed indulged in some illicit transactions, but he was handicapped by the fact that the Neora river ran along the escarpment which constituted the boundary of the valuable Sal timber tract, and the grasslands through which the timber had to be taken out were waterlogged for half the year. However, he had made a beginning, and a ford known as Chor Leek ('Robbers Path') had become a well-known entry point.

One morning we set off to look for some farmland closer to the forest and further away from human occupation. I rode Bhagwan Piari and Pincha, my faithful old mongrel dog, followed behind. We crossed a *bhagar* where the dog had to swim on occasions, biting his way through entangling weeds. The going on higher land was easier for him as he gingerly picked his way in the wake of the trampled grass left by the elephant. Coots skittered away in the occasional pools left by the flood waters, and occasionally a hogdeer rushed out, in the manner of the pig from which it derives its name. We came upon a large python coiled on a tree above the Soheli tributary, which we followed until its junction with the Neora. Above loomed the stately Sal trees on top of an escarpment, and way to the north, tier upon tier of mountains buttressed the ethereal peak of Nanda Devi. I was enchanted by the setting, the meeting of the waters, and the thought that I had reached the last bastion in my retreat from human settlements.

I leased 173 acres of land, and started clearing operations. Trees had to be dug out and huge roots pulled away by my crawler tractor and Bhagwan Piari. The area was subject to large-scale flooding during the monsoon, largely because enough outlet spans had not been constructed on the embankment of the railway, and partly because the meandering course of the river was choked by fallen timber each year. This condition was further aggravated when the construction of a metal road took place and the engineer in charge reduced the outlet spans from three to two in revenge after a Wildlife Warden and I had caught him poaching. It took me five years to shore the various cutaways into my farmland, as the embankments kept on collapsing and had to be rebuilt. My original approach to Tiger Haven, which I had originally called after my Air Force brother who was also known as Tiger, was over a tree which had fallen across the river. Later, I constructed a fairweather road connection. In the mean time I built myself another small one-room straw hut instead of the concrete structure it had taken me fourteen years to build at Jasbirnagar, and I was ready to start again.

I now lost Pincha. He was sixteen and a quarter, but his indomitable heart would not be stilled. He rolled down the bank of the river which he had swum in so often, and was too weak to get out, and there I found him. He was the founder member of the Tiger Haven Cemetery in which he has a headstone.

Retreating before the advance of cultivation, the swampdeer had now colonized Ghola, a 3,000-acre plot of grassland owned by L.D.W. Hearsey, and now under lease to three farmers. But a sword of Damocles hung over these leaseholders as well, for a ceiling on the possession of land was soon to be imposed by the government, and the area would then vest in the State. The land configuration of Ghola was in the shape of a cup, with a lake in the centre. We had estimated that about 1,500 swampdeer occupied this area, which adjoined the Reserved Forest Grassland of Sathiana. Bounded by the Neora which flowed along the escarpment about 50 feet high, a forest of Sal extended to the Nepal border. This formed the last refuge for the swampdeer of the marshy plains.

The State Board of Wildlife was constituted in 1964, and I was appointed a member. I submitted a resolution proposing that, in view of the fact that Ghola would lapse to the government with the imposition of a ceiling on land holdings, the 3,000 acres contiguous to the Reserved Forest, which seemed to be the last stronghold of the endangered swampdeer, should be taken into the North Kheri Forest Division. The Chief Wildlife Warden came to visit me and together we went round the area. We visited the Ghola lake where dessicated carcases of wounded animals who had come to the water to die lay submerged. The Chief Wildlife Warden left with great expressions of sympathy, and a seeming determination that something had to be done.

However, nothing transpired, and the arable land was gradually taken over by Naxalites and other landgrabbers. As the position continued to worsen, I determined to take matters into my own hands and try to entice the recalcitrant barasinghas into the Reserved Forest where they would be comparatively safe. For though their flesh was comparatively unpalatable there was a growing market for meat. I ploughed up some forest land under strong protest from the local staff, and planted barley and constructed some salt licks. As soon as the barley started sprouting I borrowed five elephants from a local shikar outfitters' establishment and staged a round-up towards the Reserved Forest. Some broke back, but the main herd which George

Schaller had estimated at 600 earlier on crossed the Soheli and entered the precincts of the forest. Next day I was gratified to see a herd of about 450 grazing in the Sathiana Meadow.

However, the herd was greatly outnumbered by domestic cattle which lived in the grassland, and from which the Forest Department received a subsidy. With the cooperation of a sympathetic Divisional Forest Officer I set fire to the temporary hutments of the cattle station, and soon the barasingha were in and the cattle out. I watched with intense satisfaction as the number grew, and in 1972, after the IUCN Meeting of the General Assembly in 1969, Colin Holloway, their Chief Ecologist, visited me and estimated 1,200–1,600 animals in the Madrahia-Sathiana complex.

Though the swampdeer had colonized the area into which they had been driven, it was not prime habitat as far as they were concerned. They would migrate out of the Madrahia-Sathiana area towards cultivation, impelled by vicious biting flies, coarse grasses and the fact that the flooding of the grassland took place in the direction of cultivation, and away from the main forest on the escarpment —all of which coincided with their fawning. As a contrast, in the case of swampdeer occupation further east, where the flooding was towards the Reserved Forest, swampdeer herds would often be found in the Sal forest during the monsoon. Additionally, as their fawning period was May to July, this voluntary shift towards high land was an attempt to safeguard the highly vulnerable fawns, which returned in depleted numbers in January or February after the grasses were burnt, having run the gauntlet of high floods and poachers' bullets.

A further catastrophe now overtook the endangered swampdeer, when they were supposedly in sight of complete environmental protection. Dudhwa had been declared a National Park, and a Managing Committee, with the senior bureaucrat of the State, appointed as Chairman. The Secretary of the Irrigation Department, as a member of the Committee, proposed that an irrigation barrage should be constructed on the Soheli river which formed the boundary of the Park. I submitted a strong note to the Chairman saying that the swampdeer, for whose conservation the Park had primarily been declared, would be greatly endangered. The very sympathetic Chairman agreed, and noted in the minutes that no structure of any description would be made on the Soheli. All seemed to be well, and the deer population continued to multiply.

However, I was unaware of the way the government functioned, and the enemy bided their time. The previous Chairman was no sooner transferred than the Irrigation Department started work on a barrage immediately outside the Park in the buffer zone. By the time the Park authorities discovered this construction, they claimed to have spent Rs 90,000, and, according to them, were unaware of the ruling which forbade the construction of the barrage. They pointed out the great financial loss which the State exchequer would be put to if the construction was abandoned. This story was accepted by the new Chairman, and when the Irrigation Department further compounded its duplicity by offering to construct safety walls, its work was allowed to proceed despite my strong protests. It seems that for governments ignorance of the law is an excuse for a fresh beginning.

From the 1,200–1,600 evaluated by Holloway, barasingha numbers are down to about 150 in the Madrahia-Sathiana area. High flood levels manipulated by the closure of the barrage outlets ensured that Tiger Haven had two and a half feet of water inside its tenements in mid-June 1988, when I also became an endangered species in my own country. It is doubtful whether the swampdeer will recover from the disaster in a hurry.

When Balram came on a visit from Calcutta in 1960 we went for a drive in the forest. There seemed to be more people than ever inside the forests on various errands, and we saw fewer animals than humans. It was dark, and we sat down to a cup of tea besides a log fire. A lapwing called across a depression, and soon after a leopard gave a succession of sawing grunts. He was objecting to the invasion of his territory. I drove my jeep to the edge of the depression, and saw in the glow of the headlights a lambent green pinpoint of light moving at right angles to our front. Resting my elbows on my knees I took careful aim from between the headlights at the moving pinpoint, and fired a shot. There was no sound, but the light went out. I advanced to the spot, and in the flashlight saw a leopard lying on the ground. A crimson circle welled behind the shoulder and, even as I watched, the fire faded from his eyes. I had brought off a spectacular shot, and acquired a fine trophy, but I felt nothing but an awful confusion—futility at the destruction of beauty and the taking of life for personal pleasure. I put aside my rifle as my father had done many years before. Soon after, the arrival of Prince, of whom I have written elsewhere, changed my life for ever.

4 Hunting

THIS treatise is an ultimate book on maneaters, not because I have any special qualification to pen the last word on this controversial subject, but because historically and temporally I am positioned to catalogue authoritatively the last stand of the tiger. Down the ages, as the dominant species we have treated the great carnivores with scant respect. We have maligned an evolution which has attained a specialist perfection over sixty million years into a subject for professional hunters with sophisticated weapons, and equated the carnivores' natural search for prey with our trophy-hunting vandalism. We have thus sought to destroy a sublime species in a fierce competitive urge which endeavours to desecrate the ultimate in perfection. The vandal who would raze the Taj Mahal to the ground in preference to the levelling of a public urinal would be in line for a prison sentence for the desecration of a national monument. Yet a Maharaja who massacred 1,157 tigers was treated as one of the great shikaris of a vanished era, and J.A. Hunter who slaughtered 1,600 rhinos was a pioneer settler of Africa.

As a descendant from the hominids who grubbed for tubers and climbed trees in search for fruit, we have now evolved into the thinking homo sapiens, who selectively feed on nightingale tongues, and wear clothes manufactured from unborn seal pup skins. But we are not the instinctive hunters we pretend to be, nor can the so-called hunting instinct be an excuse for the heedless battues which gunned down prime stags for their trophy antlers while abandoning the carcasses to scavengers and debasing the breeding herds.

In a very few years we have plundered our planet of riches manufactured over the millennia by bacterial action on fossil plants, and animal relicts. We have exploited the coal seams and the oil wells to a point of diminishing return. We search for alternative sources of power, but the nuclear energizers largely propel warheads, missiles and nuclear- powered battleships. By the Star Wars initiative we seek to extend internecine struggles into the fourth dimension, and soon we may fulfil tradition when Mars comes into its own. Our denuded and exploited hillsides pour silt into massive dams built in a megalomaniacal splurge, choking their utility. We are felling forests, displacing age-old civilizations, and rendering their future both destructive and infructuous. The ecological crisis whereby cultivation and civilization are devastated by floods is sought to be remedied not by damming the errant river, but by tree plantations to hold the collapsing hills—not because of any desire to recompense nature for the piracy we have committed, but because of a terror of the finality of the reprisals that nature has in store.

Yet when habitat and prey species are destroyed and the tiger kills a human, the ecological crisis is solved by the declaration of a maneater for not obeying man-made laws, for that is the easiest solution. Such is the scale of values vis-à-vis wildlife. John Aspinall succinctly says: 'Man has forgotten that we owe everything to Nature. The totality is manifest, our willingness to pay back anything on account barely discernible. Our only solution is to steal more and more of her dwindling resources and feed them into the industrial boiler, while hoping it will blow up in the next generation.' It is certain that the human niche in nature's evolutionary process will leave the universe a degraded memorial to our rapacity, and the ruptured planet will tremble at our ponderous retreating footfall.

As the dominant living species on earth, man has devised religions that apportion the fate of lesser evolutionary creatures to his mercy. The Christian religion, which has made us in the image of God has the audacity to give us dominion over the birds and the beasts. The Moslems claim that many animals are unclean, and only a few are worthy of human consumption. Other creeds maintain the sanctity of human life, implying the opposite for other life forms; and all claim the supremacy of the human race. Sport killing and habitat reclamation has brought countless animals to extinction, and countless more will follow, until the human stands on a deserted pinnacle, for a brief moment of splendour, until he joins the Gadarene rush. *Sic transit Gloria Mundi.*

Of all the ploys which humanity has initiated, or employed, sport hunting is the most sinful, the most apocryphal, and the most hypocritical—an act which is opposed to civilized human thought, whereby man enjoys murder for his own entertainment. The supposed natural law of might is right, by which the human has usurped the world which he increasingly claims, is opposed to the edict of live and let live which normally prevails among wild animals.

Killing for pleasure is inhibited by intra-specific laws, but the mass genocide of animals is permissible under the guise of 'sport hunting'. Hitler endeavoured to perpetuate the anathema of the *Herrenvolk* which the world community rebelled against, but, though eight subspecies of tiger have emerged out of Siberia, our world scientists refuse to countenance a mixing of the subspecies to obtain a genetic viability, even though they emanate from the same genetic stock; they would rather perpetuate the dogma of racial purity, so discredited in the case of human beings. The crime of genocide is squarely on the scientists whereby they advocate racial purity for animals, while a constriction of habitat in a territorial animal leads to a population depletion and degradation through inbreeding. Hybridization vitalizes plant genetics, but subspecies of animals are encouraged to inbreed!

Alas, the ethos of sport killing is a virus so deeply embedded in the human psyche that it is not possible to exorcise the immorality of taking the life of an animate process of evolution for the sake of individual pleasure. The human has evolved in a similar manner from other life forms in existence today, and it is reprehensible even to consider that technological sophistication enables him to slaughter a progenitor to satisfy an insatiable longing for selective destruction. Yet such is the finality with which mass murder is condoned that hunting in the dictionary definition is equated with the search for prey or sport. So ingrained is the so-called hunting ethic in human psychology that the desire for ritualized destruction is supported by political lobbies in developed countries and commercial organizations in 'Third World' countries, who watch wealthy foreigners sport-killing indigenous game animals without any return to the local inhabitants. This ultimately becomes the genesis for the poaching racket with its multi-million dollar affiliations and the use of sophisticated firearms. Richard Leakey, a distinguished expatriate in charge of wildlife in Kenya, has been instrumental in destroying $ 2.5 million worth of ivory and $ 5 million worth of confiscated rhino horn to demonstrate that wildlife artifacts have no legal value, and to destroy a market which is banned to poachers, but legalized for government auctions. Yet, as a precedent, a President of Kenya ordered a similar consignment delivered to his wife.

However, the most degrading manifestation of it all is the acceptance of sport hunting by world conservation organizations. Such acquiescence by prominent conservation bodies implies the legalization of killing for pleasure. It is an exploitation of the assets of poor countries by the affluent ones, and of wildlife—which must pay for its own preservation. Such world institutions should come out into the open against sport killing, but the IUCN seems favourably inclined towards quotas for the cheetah in Africa, claiming that a 'sustained yield' may offer conservation incentives to private landholders. Leopard' quotas are sought on the basis of computer censuses in East Africa, and even Nepal, which has hardly any habitat left, has applied for a 'leopard quota'. It is shameful that incentives have to be offered by committed organizations to preserve endangered species, and it will be obvious to any thinking person looking into a crystal that such an outlook merely delays extinction but at the same time confirms it. The entire attitude of humanity towards other creations must be drastically revised. Sport killing must be declared illegal. Apart from the ethics of killing, it is against all the laws of civilized equity that a millionaire can invade a foreign country and trophy hunt in another land on the strength of his wealth, while the local inhabitant, who starves for protein, cannot find sustenance in the country of his origin.

But let us examine the canard that has endowed the human with a so-called hunting instinct which now governs the social ethos, influences conservation policy in legislatures, and is generally accepted as the basis of aberrant behaviour in human activities. The closest relations of humans today are the great apes: the gorillas, chimpanzees and orang-utans. Their intelligence is phenomenal, and it is suggested that up to the age of eight the chimp has greater powers of concentration than a human child of the same age. David Taylor, a zoo vet, was surprised when Henri a chimpanzee picked him up on a motorcycle and took him from a hotel in Marseilles to the ape house at the zoo! The gorillas and the solitary orang are more introverted, but have similar IQs which often astonish their human associates. They are anatomically similar to the human, but there is no reliable record of the gorilla eating meat in the wild, though they will readily do so in captivity. The extroverted chimpanzee is an opportunistic meat eater, and Jane Goodall relates that they will kill young deer and devour it with relish, but as far as daily forage goes the apes are essentially frugivororous and herbivorous. The dentures of prehistoric man bear a striking resemblance to that of apes in their prognathous jaws and receding cranium, and the gorilla often has a prominent saggital crest.

It is therefore likely that the human became a compulsive meat eater at a later stage of evolution, when other factors intervened to convert him into becoming a selective feeder. The acquisition of, and ability to use, weapons and tools to subdue and carve large prey animals enabled him to capture animals. Thereafter, as more efficient weaponry became available and fire was discovered, man became omnivorous because of a greater selectivity in dietary demands. Though he has become a carnivore through choice, he cannot justifiably claim through sophistry or legerdemain that he is a hunter by instinct, or that he is impelled by the same compulsions as the descendants of the legendary sabre tooth and the nimravines, who have attained their present-day specialist perfection in the forms of the tiger, lion, jaguar, leopard, the mountain lion, cheetah, and many forms of smaller cats and predators ordained by nature to prey or perish. Given the fact that man is not a hunter by instinct, and in view of the present precarious balance of the human vis-à-vis animal population, it is obvious and essential that we outlaw the belief that holds sport hunting to be a recreational occupation. Recognizing the immense hold that this recreational murder has on the psyche of the human race, the first to do so should be international conservation bodies.

The proposed commercial hunting of the Snow Leopard (*Panthera Uncia*) and Argali Sheep (*Ovis Ammon*) in Mongolia by a hunting organization in the United States on the grounds that they are killing off too many sheep and ibex is an act of criminality and hypocrisy which should be condemned by responsible conservationists throughout the world. It highlights all the base and fraudulent claims of the hunters' lobby and their so-called concern for endangered species; and their tongue-in-cheek talk of sustained yields and quota culling will provide a loophole with which to evade the prohibition of trade in endangered species. The legalized hunting of species competitive to man is an unwarranted exploitation by affluent foreigners; and for an endangered species, which is always under strong pressure from local human opposition, as is the Snow Leopard, it is a regressive and negative approach that should be totally repudiated by international forums. Nowhere in the world is the Snow Leopard found in large numbers and it is highly questionable whether the Mongolian or United States wildlife authorities are correct in saying that an over-abundance of Snow Leopards is killing too many sheep and ibex. In any case, it is obvious from an advertisement that the main desire is to hunt the Argali Sheep as well, and the Snow Leopard supposedly competes with this desire. What is the yardstick for deciding that there is over-abundance or 'too many' in an accepted high-altitude population which is always low? And might not the pressure of sport hunters have combined to divert the Snow Leopard to predation on domestic stock, which, of course, is unacceptable to the subsistence-level stock breeder? The Snow Leopard is an Indicator Species of the health of high-altitude wildlife populations, and wishful estimates of 'sustained yields' by wealthy foreign entrepreneurs, and their acceptance by local wildlife authorities, is the beginning of the end. As George Schaller, the distinguished scientist and conservationist, says: 'For epochs to come, the peaks will still pierce the lonely vistas, but when the last Snow Leopard has stalked among the crags and the last markhor has stood on a promontory, his ruff waving in the breeze, a spark of life will have gone, turning the mountains into stones of silence.'

Once killing for sport has been outlawed, a firm basis for future action will have been evolved, and it will be acknowledged that man has no right to destroy what he cannot create. Licensed killing is the thin edge of the wedge which increasingly justifies illegalities. When the affluent pay large sums to kill animals, and the financial proceeds go into the coffers of rich entrepreneurs, resentment grows among local inhabitants in direct competition with local wildlife because they do not benefit from the income derived therefrom. The involvement of the local population in commercial poaching stems from this resentment, and sport hunters often act as a cover for such illegal activities, increasing the difficulties of the over-burdened protection staff. If sport killing becomes a crime under any circumstances, no benefit-of-doubt could or would work to the advantage of the slaughterer—just as the Criminal Procedure Code does not justify murder under any circumstances.

The slaughter of members of evolutionary processes for sport is a crime against posterity. Extinction comes to a species for extremely valid reasons, and life forms evolve morphologically into other shapes more adapted to habitat conditions, for nature's infinite wisdom is adaptable and not wasteful. When many of the great dinosaurs, pushed by the ice ages and loss of habitat, passed into limbo, a great many evolved into lesser forms and still survive. Under the wisdom of natural conditions extinction comes but rarely, but now under the baleful influence of human occupation, one life form or more may go every year, and one never knows when Armageddon will take over.

Sport killing is deeply entrenched in a 'macho' human psyche. It is an all-male occupation, and boosts the male ego. The basically immoral precept of maiming and killing for pleasure, the orphaning of young and helpless progeny, the massacre of groups to capture individuals, has been romanticized to the selfish cliché that it is the chase which matters and not the kill. But no amount of hypocritical persuasion can justify the killing of an animate creation. Means cannot justify ends, however much the latter are romanticized.

Kipling romanticized the hunt thus:

'Do you know the long day's patience, belly-down on frozen drift,
While the head of heads is feeding out of range?
It is there that I am going, where the boulders and the snow lie,
With a trusty nimble tracker that I know.
I have sworn an oath, to keep it on the Horns of Ovis Poli,
And the red gods call me out and I must go.'

Robert Ruark, the author of *Uhuru and Other African Tales*, writing in the manner of Hemingway, observed with sheer arrogance:

This was a very fine Simba, this last lion that I shall ever shoot. He had this real red mane as red as Ann Sheridan's and bright green eyes. . . . He was the handsomest lion I had ever seen in or out of a zoo, and I was not sorry, about the collection of him. Already I was beginning to fall into the African way of thinking: that if you properly respect what you are after, and shoot it cleanly and on the animal's terrain, if you imprison in your mind all the wonder of the day, from sky to smell to breeze to flowers—then you have not merely killed an animal. You have lent immortality to a beast you have killed because you loved him, and wanted him for ever, so that you could always recapture the day. You could always remember how blue the sky was, and how you sat on the high hill under the umbrella of the mimosa. This is better than letting him grow a few years older, to be killed or crippled by a son, and eaten still alive by hyenas. Death is not a dreadful thing in Africa.

But even these men who went to seek the Holy Grail of hunting had their own code. They gunned for the best, the most dangerous, and the most beauteous. The 'Big Five' of Africa, the elephant, the rhino, the Cape Buffalo, the leopard and the lion were matched by equivalents in India, but they were all pursued with the objective of slaughter. They were studied over the sights of a rifle and false, aggressive and regressive portraits began to emerge. Interminable 'macho' discussions took place as to which was the most dangerous when wounded. The leopard was branded 'unpredictable' when he was merely smart enough to turn the tables on a pursuer when wounded. The buffalo supposedly doubled on his tracks to take his oppressor in the rear. The elephant charged like a screaming flail out of hell, the lion a coughing haystack bent on destruction. Colonel Glasfurd called the tiger a gentleman, and the leopard a bounder—an epithet usually reserved for humans in their dealings with each other—but Glasfurd was mauled by a leopard he had wounded. The hunters' intrinsic code insisted that they follow an animal to put it out of its misery, though it was they who had been the cause of the misery. Many were mauled in retaliation by these potentially dangerous animals, and some were killed in the performance of what they considered to be the obligation of sport hunting. This was the acme of sport killing, though the sacrifice of a life is basically immoral.

The tough, staccato style of Ernest Hemingway, one of the greatest writers of our generation, is peculiarly suited to romanticizing sport killing. He nevertheless fails to evaluate the ethic of the heartless brutality which deprives an animate and feeling being of the right to exist. In *The Short Happy Life of Francis Macomber* Hemingway describes in gruesome, powerful detail how a majestic lion was almost pulverized by hunters. First, the lion 'heard a cracking crash and felt the slam of a 30–06 ·220-grain solid bullet that bit his flank, and ripped in sudden scalding nausea through his stomach.' Then 'it crashed again and he felt the blow as it hit his lower ribs and ripped on through the blood suddenly hot and frothy in his mouth.' Riddled with pain and gaping wounds the lion 'galloped towards the high grass where he could crouch and not be seen and make them bring the crashing thing close enough so he could make a rush and get that man that held it . . . his tail stiffened to twitch up and down, and as they came into the edge of the grass, he made a coughing grunt and charged.' Macomber panicked and fled into the open, but three more bullets were fired into the animal by his companions and the 'crawling, heavy yellow bulk of the lion stiffened and the huge, mutilated head slid forward and Macomber stood by himself in the clearing where he had run, holding a loaded rifle, while two black men and a white looked at him in contempt, knew that the lion was dead.' Hemingway was a master of his craft, and in this episode he brings out the pseudo-heroics, cynical brutality, and overweening arrogance involved in the needless agony and destruction of a symbol that epitomizes the acme of sport hunting which has gripped the human psyche. Yet even Hemingway is unable to present an apologia or *raison d'etre* in taking life for a vandal's pleasure.

Methods of hunting have been further debased and sport hunting has become a status symbol, a subject of animated discussion on the cocktail circuit, and a part of the competitive numbers game whereby the Maharaja of Sarguja's score was matched by the Maharaja of Rewa till 500. Later, Rewa's son became a conservationist, but old-man Sarguja claimed a score of 1,157, including unborn foetuses, to put up the numbers slaughtered by him; and so down the line. We have poachers, flashlights, car shooters, and commercial killers. But they all aspire now to shoot the best and the most dangerous with the least effort. The human ego incites a person to indulge in feats of vandalism to prove his mettle, for destruction provides a far greater *illusion* of power and ability than conservation or creation.

A tree can be felled in a matter of minutes and falls with a great crash, destroying lesser shrubs growing in its shadow. The impact is cataclysmic. Yet a tree grows imperceptibly, it has to be nurtured carefully, and there is no fanfare when it reaches maturity, but life is born. A tiger or leopard is shot as a maneater because it has been driven to killing a human with the destruction of its habitat and natural prey species. The man who destroys them is eulogized and rewarded, but a man who endeavours to save their life by providing them with sustenance, is said to go against natural processes of elimination.

The human ego needs perpetual fuelling and is in reality a way of battling an inferiority complex. When man destroys a powerful animal he has brought about the downfall of something stronger than himself and thereby boosted his faltering ego. If he does so with a super-sophisticated firearm, he employs a weapon more effective than that of his competitive neighbour. In relation to sport killing the human ego is a strangely complicated phenomenon which relates to a competitive ploy embracing a whole gamut of emotions, and should be written up by a psychiatrist.

The attitudes to sport hunting in Africa have always appeared to be more liberal and chivalrous than those in Nepal, India and South-east Asia. Perhaps this is because they have been chronicled mainly by selected expatriates and visiting sportsmen, for the dubious methods used by local inhabitants and poachers are the same in all 'Third World' countries. The affluent and millionaires who seek the Holy Grail in developing countries, return to the hunting lobbies of their own nations to proclaim the need to save the glamorous preda-tors, but only in others' countries, so that they may go and hunt them there. The lynx, reintroduced into Switzerland, has a very doubtful future. The wolves and the bears are memories in Europe, and the mountain lion clings precariously to existence in the United States.

The predators are maligned everywhere but in reality they lead exemplary lives. Wolves control their population not only by seasonal breeding, but also because only the Alpha Male sires a family. They live on seasonal prey, and Farley Mowat discovered that the blame attributed to the wolf for the decimation of caribou herds in Canada was false. In reality the overkilling by Eskimos was responsible, and the vilified wolves subsisted on field rats and other rodents during the lean periods. Konrad Lorenz speaks of the submissive attitude of wolves and comments: 'The chivalry of a wolf has enlightened me: not so that your enemy may strike you again do you turn the other cheek, but to make him unable to do so.' Despite all the evidence to the contrary, the wolf is always big and bad in nursery tales, and it devoured Little Red Riding Hood's grandmother. Traditionally, the tiger is depicted as being ferocious and a potential maneater, and even that hunter naturalist, Dunbar Brander, talks of the lustful pleasure the tiger takes in killing when, in reality, he is ordained by nature to subsist on flesh and has merely perfected his killing skill.

The processes by which tigers control their populations are made out by people with little knowledge to suggest ravening monsters. The male is supposed to devour his offspring if given a chance. In reality infanticide is against the laws of nature, and when a male takes over a territory he will destroy the progeny of the previous ruler to induce the bereft môther to come into season and ensure a familial heirarchy, thus obviating the possibility of a future challenge. It is also believed that tigers fight to the death over tigresses in season. Yet I have observed how, when Tara's Male mated with the Median Tigress, Long Toes, the other occupant of the Range, did not interfere with his activities, though he was fully aware of what was going on and had, in fact, chased Tara's Male a few days earlier after a scuffle over a kill. Schaller also relates how a lion mated while his companion sat watching fifty metres away, but when he tranquillized the mating lion his companion took over.

It is unfortunate that the human, who cannot control his own procreation, has used essential biological differences to condemn for his own purposes the wisdom that nature has selectively evolved.

Over the years, feudal rulers have preserved the great cats—not because they were conservationists, but because they wanted to be able to pursue them for sport. When Armand Denis, a veteran TV producer, visited the King of Nepal, he pointed to a number of rhino heads garishly arrayed on the walls of his throne room; when he suggested that there were very few Great Indian Rhinos left in existence, he was told with a wink from His Majesty that they would probably last his lifetime! But the rhino was chiefly hunted in the Hindu kingdom because of the ceremonial religious rite of Khudga Rudhir Tarpan, whereby the person offering a blood libation to his ancestor while standing in the disembowelled rhino carcass would supposedly be spared the various transmigrations of the soul on its way to Nirvana. It is worthwhile examining how sport hunting operated in Nepal, and its impact on the present.

The Kingdom of Nepal abuts the northern boundary of India for its entire length of 540 miles. A hundred miles in width, it lies between 80° and 88° longitude and 26° and 30° degrees latitude, and it is hemmed in by the two huge countries of India and China. Bountifully endowed by nature, its great mountain system runs almost parallel to its entire length. Comprising the highest peaks in the world, the Himalaya have twenty-six peaks of over 24,000 feet, including twelve over 25,000, eight over 26,000, three over 27,000, and the one and only Everest, a challenge to all mountaineers. The Mahabharata Range runs along this stretch of the snow clad mountains, and further to the south stretches the Churia Range of hills, the last rampart of the Himalaya rising to a height of 2,400 feet. Here we have tier upon tier of wild, broken country intersected by ravines and marshy streams and with a rainfall of 100 inches annually. Towering trees and creeper-clad undergrowth shade the ultimate and selective breeding grounds of the tiger. This was a permanent source of supply for the more disturbed forests of India. To the south of the foothills lies the Charkesia Jhari, or Eight-mile Forest, merging into the Tarai forests of India. Known as the Bhabar and consisting of detritus washed down from the hills, and overlaid with pebbles, sand and boulders, with shallow intersecting streams where flash floods predominate, it is unfit for cultivation.

The great river systems of Nepal emerge from these hills and mountains, and flow into India. To the east is the basin of the seven Kosis, drained by their tributaries. To the centre is the tract drained by the seven Gandaks, i.e. the Gandak, the Narayani and its great tributaries. To the west are the Karnali (Ghagra) and Mahakali (Sarda) rivers. Caught up in the last spasm of the Himalayan uplift a few million years ago, these unstable hills were protected by virgin forest—the home of a seemingly unending supply of tigers and leopards, and the hunting grounds of the rulers of Nepal. The area provides unmatched views of mountain peaks surrounded by swirling mist, and has a vast river system where Gangetic Dolphins once gambolled in mid-stream and Marsh Crocodiles and Gharials basked on the sandbanks.

Maharaja Jung Bahadur Rana, the originator of organized hunting in Nepal, started the Ring System. During his regime in the early years of the twentieth century as many as seven hundred elephants were employed in a shoot. Buffalo baits were tied up and, if there was a kill, trained shikaris or trackers were sent off to locate the tiger. The elephants then moved in and surrounded the grass or forest where the tiger was supposed to be lying. The circumference of the circle got smaller as the elephants moved in, until ultimately all retreat was cut off. The stauncher and selected elephants would then move into the ring, and the tiger, his retreat out off, would charge the line of elephants, to be met with shouts and missiles until it appeared in front of the person who was supposed to shoot. Sometimes the tiger broke through, and to prevent such an occurrence, Jang Bahadur would personally belabour the offending *Filwan* or Mahawat with his stick! It thus became a point of discretion as well as honour for the elephants to prevent such an escape.

As elephant numbers dwindled, Maharajah Joodha Shamshere Jung, Jang Bahadur's successor, introduced innovations whereby the Ring of elephants was supplemented with strips of white cloth to contain the tigers. This system not only made do with fewer elephants, but also made it possible to operate more than one ring, for tigers with their inborn suspicion of the unfamiliar did not willingly cross the cloth curtain. Joodha Shamshere, mounted on a staunch elephant with a howdah would advance into the Ring, supported by an elephant on either side and three or four elephants forming a skirmishing line in front. As soon as the tigers were located, the line withdrew, leaving the hunter to face the quarry in the Ring, which on occasions contained six tigers. The primordial setting of almost impenetrable forests, of grasses twice as high as the skirmishing elephants, the thunderous challenge of more than one charging tiger, the trumpeting and squeals of panic-stricken elephants, and the whiplash crack of cordite gave an elemental quality to the inferno. As the raging tigers fought back, they sprang on to the heads of the pachyderms and pulled them to their knees. The great tuskers crushed them with their trunks, and tried to impale them with their tusks, and the pandemonium could only be comparable to the crash of the elements.

My father described one such hunt in Nepal in which the tiger broke out of the encircling Ring after being fired at, and bounded away in great leaps, giving vent to full-throated roars, his pads pounding the forest floor like those of a polo pony. Behind the breached Ring flowed a jungle stream into which the tiger landed in a welter of spray. As the great beast entered the forest sudden silence reigned where once there had been sound and fury. My father described the scene and action, and the sudden, uncanny cessation of noise had a dream quality which haunted him for days after its occurrence.

Though these hunts were mind-boggling in their dramatic *denouement*, the sheer cost of life for the pleasure of a feudal ruler was prohibitive enough to make the mass slaughter a sickening exhibition. In seven seasons, kills ranged from a bag of 433 tigers to 120 in a season of 68 days, and an individual daily bag could be of seven tigers. A record tiger of 10 feet 9 inches weighing 705 pounds was shot, and a leopard measuring 9 feet 4 inches. Such statistics, kept to boost the ego of a single person, are criminal. The performance of feats of daring have always captured the imagination of worthwhile people, whether it be climbing a mountain because it is there, or any other performance requiring dedication, endurance and courage. Hunting dangerous animals was once in this category, but it has now been debased as a sport with the continuous development of fire-arms, and people have found it an ever easier way of fostering an image of masculinity.

Among the last participants in a tiger hunt by the Ring method were the Maharaja of Sarguja and the Maharaj Kumar of Vizianagram, the well-known cricketer. Vizzy related to me how they had been allowed to shoot a quota of six tigers apiece and that the harrassed animals would sit panting in the noonday heat of May. To my query as to whether, as an accomplished cricketer, he would relish hitting a six off a third-rate bowler, he said in extenuation that he used to clap his hands to make the tiger move, but old Sarguja (who presumably did not play cricket) had no such scruples! Thus was the sport of hunting debased to the numbers game, where all that mattered was the total, and the inflation of a human ego by the use of sophisticated weapon-ry. Even the sometimes fatal, romantic gesture whereby a hunter followed a dangerous animal when wounded in a final confrontation was not possible, for the habitat was so impenetrable that all the advantage lay with the enraged tiger if followed by a man on foot. The tiger, the world's most powerful and glamorous predator, was at the mercy of geriatrics who merely possessed the financial ability to organize lavish hunts. The Maharaja of Sarguja topped the proverbial three score and ten by a goodly margin and possessed a lone, left eye; he shot off the right shoulder in a strange but remarkably effective contortion.

Nepal, once so lavishly endowed by nature, now stands as a monument to a raped environment. The great mammals, decimated by the mindless battues of erstwhile rulers, exist only in isolated pockets; the migration routes of the great pachyderms have been disrupted, the prey species of the predators are in short supply, and the burgeoning human population is in demographic dominance everywhere. The great timber forests have been laid waste by uncar-ing and ignorant lay rulers bent upon extracting the last revenue from them in their life time. The vast watersheds carry increasing loads of silt from the denuded mountain-sides and cause floods, the silting of dams and hydroelectric weirs, and the devastation of habitat. Only the great mountain peaks remain to pierce the lonely vistas untamed and unravished.

Robert Ruark, the touchstone of African sport hunting writes after a hunt in India: 'A dead tiger is the biggest thing I have ever seen in my life, and I have shot an elephant. A live tiger is the most exciting thing I have ever seen in my life, and I have shot a lion. A tiger in a hurry is the fastest thing I have ever seen in my life, and I have shot a leopard. A wild tiger is the most frightening thing I have seen in my life, and I have shot a Cape Buffalo. But for the sport involved, I would rather shoot quail than another tiger.'

Sport hunting has always had debased overtones in India. It is perhaps because it was indulged in by the local British rulers and the Indian feudal chiefs, who felt that the local fauna existed for their entertainment. For about twenty years after Independence shikar outfitters, mostly consisting of displaced feudal rulers who had lost their States, started using their resources and expertise in inviting wealthy foreigners to come out to India to hunt. The chief target was, of course, the tiger, and twenty-six outfitter companies opened up to start earning foreign exchange through killing our depleted wildlife. They operated under the excuse of earning much needed foreign exchange for the country. Many functioned with a guarantee of a refund if a tiger was not killed, and would sacrifice scruples to prevent such a money-back eventuality. Allwyn Cooper went to the extent of setting up a dead leopard for Ruark to hunt when they could not find a live one for him to shoot according to the rules. They used flashlights from wheeled vehicles, sat up all night over kills, went into territory not on their licenses, used poison and other nefarious methods. When the ban on tiger shooting came in 1969–70 they asked their foreign clients to write to the Government of India suggesting that they were really conservationists, as they paid money to keep out the poachers. Failing this ploy, they sanctimoniously spoke of conservation, tourism and earning money from a live tiger rather than a dead one. One shikar outfitter went to the extent of opening a camp in Indonesia and then filed a writ petition against Project Tiger in the Sunderbans: he claimed that all the tigers there were maneaters and causing untold harm to the local inhabitants. He came to Dudhwa and claimed that all the casualties of maneating were by Tara. But even these ploys were the dying spasms of unscrupulous operators.

Loss of habitat has put an end to such insensate destruction of wildlife, but hunter-outfitters still seek ways and means of exploiting the tiger. They would like to get tigers declared maneaters, and invite foreigners to pay large sums to kill these so-called aberrant animals who have refused to obey man-made laws. It can well be imagined that many animals would be declared maneaters to assist in this prostitution of wild wealth, and what methods would be used to induce such a declaration by the competent authorities. One foreign killer offered Rs 2,00,000 just for the privilege of slaying a maneating tigress. However, it is fortunate that the hunting lobby is not powerful in India, and the pantheon of Hindu gods is associated with animals. The Bishnois of Rajasthan protect the blackbuck, and the Nilgai is a relative of the sacred cow in name. The abolition of sport hunting is essential, for the easier the issuance of a licence for a particular purpose of violence becomes, the more is it liable to be used for extraneous and extempore purposes of offence. In the USA the ease of licensing has lead to the assassination of Presidents, and in India political terrorism is also spreading at a distressing rate.

The halcyon days of sport killing are however drawing to a close—not because of any change in human behaviour or outlook, but because there is nothing left to shoot, though hunters are still trying to get into the act and hunting is opening up on private lands in South Africa, and in other parts of that continent. During his study of lions in the Serengeti, George Schaller found that the animals he had painfully ear-tagged in the Park got shot if they happened to stray outside, and the hunters derisively sent him the tags. Mark and Delia Owens found the eartag of a lion they had saved from death in the trophy shed of a hunter to whom they had been describing the operation which saved the life of the predator. A hunting quota is proposed for leopards in Africa on the basis of a computer estimate, and Nepal, under pressure from the American lobby, is trying to establish a quota too. Confined to small Reserves, and in competition with the tiger, the leopard, which could seemingly adapt to any population pressure, is now possibly more endangered than the tiger who has so successfully captured the human imagination, and perhaps human emotions.

Peter Adamson, giving his views on modern hunting writes: 'Australia is tragically and brutally a professional and recreational hunter's dream. Helicopter shooting of water buffalo and wild horse. Conventional shooting of millions of kangaroo, duck, rabbits, wild goat and pig. There is a traditional saying: "If it moves, shoot it: If it doesn't, cut it down." ' Nowhere has sport killing been more debased than in Australia. Africa and Asia have offered the slaughter of dangerous animals in the form of the 'Big Five', and this exercise has produced thrills of the chase and the euphoria of the kill. At least it involves the expertise of the hunt, and the real danger of the hunter meeting his end, with the tables being turned. But in Australia, where no dangerous game exists, feral animals like the buffalo and horse are massacred with sophisticated firearms with all the panoply, panache and lavish expenditure of the African Safari.

Adamson writes further: 'Hunters often assert that man (not women it seems) must be able to express his natural instincts. This argument justifies what he—man—regards as natural instincts. As such it not only can be, but has been used to justify rape, abduction, enslavement of women and children, plunder, vandalism, or the modern equivalent of whatever whim man has.' The fact that very few women hanker after sport hunting is a significant pointer in determining whether it is the hunting instinct which motivates the human to slaughter wild creatures or whether it is a baser compulsion with psychiatric connotations which impels the 'he-man' to utilize his sophistry in the pursuit of other natural creations. A few ladies may take pleasure in killing for a variety of reasons but, by and large, feminine nature does not aspire to sport killing. A cogent analogy to illustrate the essential difference between hunting and sport killing may be found in the functioning of the lion pride. It is the lioness who is the accomplished huntress, and the males act as free loaders whose ponderous dignity ensures the integrity of the pride, yet seldom contributes to its hunting prowess. They do not kill more than their requirements, and the sight of a non-hunting lion, walking slowly in front of a line of unalarmed African antelopes, recalls a general inspecting troops under his command. But man has only to alight from his vehicle and animals start to run.

Bird shooting has been overshadowed by the reaction against the needless slaughter of more spectacular animals. But the shooting of 200 sandgrouse in a single morning in Bikaner, or of 4,000 duck in Bharatpur, as happened at Viceregal shoots, are examples of mindless, totally uncivilized massacres. We speak of putting a wounded animal out of its misery, but what about the birds that are maimed, not by one ill-aimed rifle shot, but by the routine discharge of scatter gun pellets into a covey of grouse or a flight of duck which leave more wounded than killed? The disregard for the plight of birds which cannot be picked up, and must die of lead poisoning, is totally callous. What of the lakes and pools which are contaminated by the lead pellets and spent shot which fall into the water? Many hundreds of tons of lead fall into still waters and are absorbed into the food chain. Migratory birds are the worst off, for they are ostensibly owned by no single country, but they are the biggest sufferers from the overkill, being fair game in every land which they pass through; and then they arrive to polluted waters of the previous season's discharge of lead pellets. In so-called civilized countries conditions are unspeakable. England celebrates the Glorious Twelfth (of August) on the opening day of the Grouse Season, yet the shot birds go to the European Common Market and are not consumed at home; and the same applies to the Red Deer. Buzzards, migrating from North Africa, are shot in Europe. All birds are fair game in France, Italy and Spain. How can we justifiably equate ourselves with the professional predator who kills only for food? From what atavistic ancestor do we derive our instinct for hunting and killing?

The outlawing of sport killing by world conservation bodies is essential. So many pressures have built up against the survival of wild animals that a drastic stand is mandatory. Unless killing for sport is outlawed, and the illegality of killing is established as an offence, restraining poaching or hunting will remain a semantic exercise. Sport killing must be treated as a heinous crime.

Habitat manipulation and management can be misapplied in the present context of habitat degradation. A deficit biomass count can become a surplus one through a dishonest process of habitat reduction, and there is much danger of this coming about in a democratic set up when there is so much demand for land. An artificial surplus is the initial step towards the creation of sport quotas and 'sustained yields' whereby an endangered species may be sport culled, as is happening in Mongolia with the Snow Leopard. Such processes could be reduced to a *reductio ad absurdum* in uncaring societies. Considering the changed circumstances in wildlife conservation, anthropomorphism must give way to a more emotional outlook in which animal behaviour should be equated with human reactions, for conservation has already in many cases given place to preservation. Wildlife can only be saved by a crusade. The rigid dogma of the scientist must be replaced by the emotive concept of the conservationist.

Anthropomorphism is an archaic and invidious concept by which the human has aspired not only to apotheosis, but has conspired to distance himself from the animal world. The human has a pregnancy, the animal has a gestation. We give birth, the animal litters. The animal trait is brutality, man is distinguished by humanity. In fact, animals merely differ from the human as regards the intelligence quotient, and even here the great apes, dolphins, and the whales have primary intellects. It is only because man wishes to dominate and exploit the natural world that he has imposed these euphemistic distinctions on the bodily functions of animals which are essentially the same as his own, and thereby transformed killing them into a pastime. A denial of animal rights terms the deliberate slaughter of other animal forms as hunting, whereas that of one human by another is murder. This false principle has contributed to our regarding the animal as a lesser breed of creation, which is really only so according to evanescent human standards and not the eternal and evolutionary one which is the eventual touchstone.

A wildlife management ploy, which is of immense harm to wildlife, is culling. Managers maintain this is essential in certain cases to maintain the biomass population in relation to the habitat available, and in preventing population pressures from degrading the habitat. In other words, the human has arrogated to himself the task of adjusting the wildlife population to the forage available in a given area. In these days of habitat reclamation for human use, this places an unwarranted onus on the human species, which, as we have already seen, is singularly unqualified to deal with population control.

Wild animals are eminently adaptable, and if certain ungulates overgraze the forage they have been used to, they will opt for other forms of life maintenance. Browsers may become grazers, and other sources may be discovered. The hardground swampdeer of Madhya Pradesh are genetically the same as the marsh inhabitants of Kaziranga. The sambhar, supposed to be solitary inhabitants of dense forest, now gregariously feed on water plants in Ranthambore, like the barasingha. Wild elephants propagate trees from the seed pods they ingest. When they cannot strip bark from trees, they switch to a diet of grass. Yet in Africa it is maintained that they have destroyed and are destroying their habitat, and should be culled for their own good. This reprehensible idea is implemented by the slaughter of entire herds in Zimbabwe, and is a crime against laws of the universe as ordained by nature. These insensate massacres are a greater offence than that of a country like Japan, which may illegally smuggle ivory, but whose artisans have never seen an elephant.

The human should now confine himself to improving the surviving habitat for animals, and securing their protection from poachers. Nature in her infinite wisdom will ensure that only the fittest survive—the ungulates by adapting to the forage availability, and the predators by their territorial demands and prey obtainable. The criminality of culling for sport or otherwise must be abrogated to place the onus of population adjustment to the processes of control by mother nature. Animals are inured to a regimen of feast or famine, and death by drought or starvation are modalities of population control. The stoicism in the acceptance of death by animals is matched by the terror of the hereafter by humans.

Sport hunting has no place in conservation forums. It places a justiciable legality on killing for pleasure, instead of condemning outright the taking of life in all its forms. But unfortunately there is sympathy for sport hunting in the Trojan Horse of international bodies, and Prince Philip is supposed to take time off from his duties as President of WWF International to celebrate the Glorious Twelfth and similar battues, before donning once more the garb of a conservationist.

5 The Legend of the Maneater

D OWN the ages since Homo acquired the status of Sapiens he has blamed natural calamities, usually engineered by his own delinquencies, on the great predators. The cult of superstition has manifested itself in the baleful activities of werewolves and weretigers, of lion men and leopard men, of vampires, poltergeists, and other evil influences of the occult. However, with the advance of knowledge and awareness the superstitious horror with which the activities of these predators were regarded has been rationalized, but the mark of Cain still persists as a relic of ancient beliefs which will not be erased. It is still generally accepted that the Big Cats are ravening monsters, full of a blood lust, waiting their appointed time to become maneaters, and to murder them is a useful, as well as a rewarding, exercise.

It is my endeavour to prove by precept and example that, even where the great cats have sinned against the laws of man, it is because we as the master race have initially violated the laws of nature. It is now in any case very doubtful whether 'Third World' countries, where most of the larger predators still survive, can rationalize a coexistence with the big animals, because of an intense demographic competition. The great cats will then be crowded into limbo. Even the clearing of their name, which has perhaps now begun, will be the obituary to the passing of a legend.

It is fairly safe to presume that the killing of humans by tigers has always been a coexistential hazard since the beginning of recorded time—originally as a prey species, but once the social evolution was complete, as an occupational risk, when the human entered tiger territory. Once man took to living in social groups, habitat requirements of the two species separated, and the human ceased to be a natural prey. He took to wearing skins other than his own, walking erect, moving in groups, talking loudly, and visiting tiger habitat only during daylight hours, and his very unfamiliarity led the tiger to shun his presence.

Some experts on tiger behaviour have suggested that the tiger has a fear complex with regard to man which has been passed down over timeless generations of inter-relations between man and tiger. However, history does not support this contention, for up to the early years of the nineteenth century the tiger was in direct spatial competition with man, and in certain parts of India it was problematical whether man or the tiger would survive. It was only with the improvement in so-called sporting weapon technology, combined with the constriction of habitat, that the tiger reacted by retreating from human proximity. During the nineteenth and early twentieth centuries this process of readjustment continued. I recall my early years during the second and third decades of the twentieth century—along the Indo-Nepal border of the Tarai, tigers were found far from human habitation, and forests adjoining cultivation, though containing large prey populations and resident leopards, had no tigers. During this interim period the preferred breeding ground of the tiger was the submontane tract of the Churia Range in Nepal where immense grasses, a full canopy of creeper-clad forest and a hundred inches of rain shielded the selective holding ground of the tiger, isolated as it was from the human presence by the dreaded scourge of Awal or endemic malaria. From this base, tigers occupied favourable niches in the forests of India. Though immediate replacements took place from the waiting list which was continually building up in this prime area when a tiger was shot in India, there was never an attempt at further colonization of peripheral habitat, however favourable. The main deterrent to further colonization was apparently the human presence.

Forest habitat was unlimited, and the growing demands of the human population had not attained the degree of exploitation by which entire ecosystems were altered. Extensive buffer areas existed between forest and habitation. Gradually, and then with a frightening finality, tiger habitat has shrunk, buffer zones have disappeared, a massive exploitation has degraded the forests to an irreparable travesty of their former luxuriance, and the human has returned to live in the forests. With habitat destruction and degradation, and the commercial poaching of prey species, the life-style of the tiger has compulsively altered.

The end of the Second World War saw the beginning of massive reclamation schemes in Nepal, as well as land hunger and timber exploitation after the attainment of Independence by India. The Nepal habitat has virtually vanished, except for small and fragmented Reserves: over-exploitation has degraded the remaining forests, and the advance of agriculture has constricted the habitat, and now no buffer areas remain. Tigers have been crowded into a last bastion of refuge, where they are forced to live cheek by jowl with the human invader, and unless we can rationalize their existence they will soon disappear. From a selective occupancy far from the human presence, the tiger has been forced into a baleful coexistence where no expansion of space is possible, and inbreeding will soon exterminate the resident populations, already weakened by other pressures. It is against this background that we must view measures aimed at preserving the tiger.

Probably the first detailed account of maneating activities was *The Maneaters of Tsavo* written by J.H. Patterson. It was the story of two maneating lions who held up railway building activities in East Africa for almost a year in 1898. Brief and more recent accounts have been given by George Adamson and Norman Carr. In India, maneating adventures were made famous by Jim Corbett who wrote about events in the present century up to the early thirties. This was followed by Kenneth Anderson, who functioned in South India and produced a number of potboilers of dubious utility and veracity. Though it is essential to study these accounts to appreciate the nature of the maneating problem which we face at present, it must also be realized that the context was an entirely different one. The tiger was the prime target of trophy hunters, sport killers and commercial outfitters, and the false glamour attendant on its killing converted it into the most dangerous animal in the world. On the basis of the old cliché that truth is stranger than fiction, shikar story writers sought to copy the style of detective fiction authors. The gruesome killings, the subtle deductions, the narrow escapes, the breathless denouement when right triumphs over wrong, and quickness on the draw by the master detective are all matched by the intrepid hunter, whose unfaltering aim lays low the master criminal, almost as he was about to claim another victim. Can anyone deny poetic licence to the scribe, or kudos to the hunter or to Corbett, who claimed to have rescued the sanity of a community at the risk of his life by killing a ravening monster?

These writers did the tiger a disservice by emphasizing the innate savagery of a hardpressed animal. Though Corbett, who was possibly our first conservationist, expresses sympathy for the maneating tigers and leopards which he was compelled to kill, he also killed many innocent ones from an inner compulsion; but he can be described as a killer with a conscience, for he lived among so-called hunters. Corbett described maneating as the compulsive seeking of human flesh by carnivores, whatever the reason; the Champawat and Panar maneaters killed 836 persons between them, and even then, judging by the period over which they operated, they did not subsist entirely on human prey. He listed maneating as being chiefly caused by old age, rendering the tiger unable to subdue ungulate prey, or incapacity brought on by wounds. Modern experience establishes that these causes are strictly local problems, essentially aggravated by scarcity of prey species. Even a superficial examination will establish that old age by itself is not a decisive causal factor; animals, though essentially adaptable, do not automatically take to an alien diet without intense compulsion. If this were not so, we would always have a run of aged tigers eking out their terminal years on a diet of human flesh. The human is not an accepted prey species for the tiger. The human's alien habits do not belong to the environ in which the tiger seeks his living, except for those tigers who have learnt by a process of familiarization that the human is the easiest prey. Old tigers usually fade into oblivion, their waning powers unable to subdue normal prey, and their mortal remains rest for a short while in the dense undergrowth of their habitat until covered in the leaf mould of the trees that sheltered them. They then disappear forever into the forest from whence they came.

Wounds are also not an inveterate cause of maneating. A tiger caught in a gin trap and speared repeatedly in the rump pulled clear and killed two of his assailants, but he died of septaecemia and starvation five weeks later by a pond in the centre of a large inhabited village. A young tiger with his lung pierced by a porcupine quill died in similar circumstances in a populated area without harming anyone. A tigress I eventually shot had its jawbone and canine broken by a bullet, and presumably survived by scavenging, but it did not take to maneating till the bone had calloused over. Another tiger took to maneating many months after its carnassial and lower canines had been fractured by a charge of buckshot. Two tigers lived with a broken foreleg apiece for two years, next to human habitation, and never took to maneating; yet they were shot, ironically enough, as potential maneaters. Tigers are able to exist as scavengers for long periods.

To a predator, anything that moves is a prospective prey species, but their acceptance is controlled or inhibited by other constraints. The elephant is too large, the mouse too small and the human is unfamiliar. But within their prey range they have food priorities, though basically aberrant behaviour is caused by prey scarcity, and they are then seldom able to pick and choose their quarry. The fact that Tara, a tigress who lived with me for seventeen months, demonstrated her preferences, was because she was fed on a regular basis and was able to indicate what she liked more than others on certain occasions.

The fact that many of Corbett's maneaters had been injured by porcupine quills was caused by prey scarcity. When the starving predator seized the rodent with an impulsive avidity and got its paws and mouth stuck with quills it was very different from the precision with which it normally launches its attack; for well nourished tigers kill selectively. Tara killed a porcupine while she was with me, with my assistance, but had to be persuaded to eat it as the meat is dark and stringy, and an inadequate meal for a full-grown tiger. She chased one as a wild tigress but abandoned pursuit after spitting out a mouthful of quills. A tiger of my acquaintance pursued a porcupine over an acre of land, periodically plucking and spitting out mouthfuls of quills until he was able to grab it by the head. After this academic feat of killing, he abandoned it. Prince, my leopard, also killed a porcupine by diligently biding his time until he could seize the rodent by the head.

The human is not under normal circumstances identified as a prey species, but a process of familiarization through living in the same agricultural habitat, combined with a prey scarcity where the human has destroyed wild ungulate species for purposes of crop protection, can readily induce predators to attack a human. However, they will initially do so only if the person is squatting in the manner of a four-footed animal. In addition, after the killing the upright stance and configuration makes the form unfamiliar, and the tiger might abandon the corpse, or academically only eat the prominent portions, such as the genitalia in a man or the breasts of a woman. During the early days of agricultural colonization, cultivators used to treat the tiger as their best unpaid watchman as no wild ungulate would come to the crop when the great cat had passed; but soon tigers learnt the lesson of adversity, and when there was nothing else to eat they turned on man, who had already destroyed prey animals under the pretence of crop protection, for with all their sophistication the human is the easiest prey of all.

Many canards have been propagated about the taste for blood of the big cats, and the classic example is that of the lion who licked his sleeping master's hand. Soon the rasping tongue drew blood and the lion supposedly ate the master! I kept both leopards and a tiger over a period of eight years, and often the needle sharp claws drew blood as they played with me. Often did I allow them to lick the blood they had drawn, but never was there any aggressive reaction.

Compulsion and their mercurial temperament enable predators to go for long stretches without a meal, and they are only compelled by dire and prolonged necessity to indulge in so-called crimes, which even in the case of humans, supposedly made in the image of god, are a product of circumstances. Air passengers marooned in the Andes ate each other of necessity, but the survivors were not charged as cannibals. In fact, a book was written about the incident. The sugarcane field harbouring a maneater is a grim place for the poor crop owner, where terror stalks the life he risks to feed and clothe his family; but inside the field are the cubs of a tigress driven out of her natural home by excessive human intrusion. She gives birth in a cultivated crop of temporary seclusion and ersatz habitat, her milk drying because crop protection firearms have slaughtered her prey animals, and her cubs are starving. Both species need a measure of sympathy, but one gets it while the other qualifies for a bullet and the cubs starve.

The tiger, whose preservation began as that of the apex for the conservation strategy of a varied and complex biotope, has now become the symbol for the underdog, typifying the natural reaction of the ecosystem against human excesses; but he is nevertheless punished for not obeying man-made laws. When a carnivore is deprived of natural prey, it will turn to what is available. When massive hunger assails a tiger, fortified by a compulsory process of familiarization, he will turn to the human as a prey species. In the days before World War II the tiger accepted a buffer between his habitat and that of human endeavour and remained isolated; even the presence of good prey populations was not inducement enough for it to transgress this imposed barrier. But now the barriers are down, and the tiger has perforce to try and come to terms with his oppressor.

It is essential to appreciate that man cannot share space with the tiger for any length of time, for eventually a familiarity will evolve into the acceptance of man as a prey species, and nature's safety valve will become infructuous. Therefore a tiger's habitat, and the ecosystem which he represents, must remain inviolate. Wildlife areas must be rationalized for the tiger to exist in niches that are separate from the human population, for once a compromise is accepted it is the beginning of the process of attrition for the microcosm of wildlife, for a compromise is only possible between equals. The human must forever remain an intruder into wildlife areas. Whether this is possible with a developing and surging democracy will depend on whether the tiger is going to survive into the foreseeable future. The recent proposal of Project Tiger to have multiple use areas occupied by both man and tiger is a regressive measure. A rethinking is essential if the tiger has to be preserved for the future, and it is unfortunate that the Project appears to be losing direction. Man and tiger cannot share space.

The maneating tiger must not be treated as an aberrant to be eliminated as soon as possible for infringing man-made laws, but as a normal tiger that has been diverted into unnatural ways by human delinquency. Efforts to wean such an animal from habits contrary to its normal mode of existence should be a matter of policy, and not of discretion which will vary with individuals and circumstances. An expert immobilization squad with proper equipment should initially tranquillize the tiger or leopard which has lapsed into contrary ways. After an inspection as to the cause of the so-called aberration, the animal should be considered for release into some suitable area, or for a mercy killing if there is no chance of recovery from an injury or ailment. In no case should incarceration in a zoo be considered, for it is against the dignity of any animal to be confined for no fault of its own. It is the final humiliation of a free ranging predator to be caged in ghetto conditions as its powers atrophy.

Unfortunately, forestry officials, persuaded by political pressures and very incomplete knowledge, maintain that it is impossible to wean a tiger or leopard from maneating. This is incorrect for, as I have stressed, maneating is an unnatural function for the great cats, and it is only in cases of grave compulsion that they will hunt a human. Not having been placed in the position of devouring my conspecific I am unable to vouch for the delectability of human flesh, but certainly the monkey, the nearest available alternative creature to the human is, contrary to popular belief, not a priority prey for the great cats. Though both my tiger and leopards killed simians they did not display any particular predilection for the flesh. There is also no authenticated proof that maneating is passed down the generations; deliberate seeking after human flesh is simply because the familiarized predator finds humans the easiest to kill and the most prolific prey species. As an example, a family of tigers with two small cubs took to maneating because of indiscriminate poaching and burning of ambush cover on the Nepal border. They were tided over this stress period by judicious and selective baiting and, after the monsoon, the cubs were well grown youngsters and there were no further cases of man slaughter.

It is also maintained that if so-called aberrant animals are translocated, it is merely a question of transferring the maneating problem. This is demonstrably incorrect for, with other more acceptable prey animals available, the predator will not hanker after a human diet. Also, as a conjecture, human habitation in a forest smells worse than any other relic of a social gathering of other animals; it is hardly likely that a creature who leaves behind such an evil smell in his excrement will have an absorbing culinary appeal for the tigers.

Finally, it is made out that, if a predator is translocated, the tiger will run the risk of aggression by other tigers into whose territory it happens to stray. However intra-specific aggression is an accepted medium of population control among tigers, and is a continuous process in areas of optimum numbers. In any case, the chance of acceptance or rejection of a translocated tiger by the local community is surely not the business of the human who had sought to destroy it in its original habitat in any case. Better by far that the moral onus of life or death devolve on the species, where the chance of acceptance would increase the genetic diversity lacking in most of our tiger areas.

The unfortunate man-tiger conflict has to be resolved by the human, but it is not possible if the essential dignity and way of life of the animal is to be ignored. The world was made for tigers to suit their way of operating. If we are to preserve them in perpetuity, the microcosm wherein they exist must not be violated. Traffic rules are enforced in concrete jungles, and a car operator is not penalized for a defaulting pedestrian, yet there are no rules governing the entry of single persons into tiger areas. Two tigers were punished for attacking lone humans who had penetrated deep into tiger habitat in the Corbett National Park, and it is obvious that what is sauce for the goose is not sauce for the gander, especially when the goose has the vote.

The present maneating phenomenon cannot be equated with the compulsive and selective preying on humans described by Corbett and Patterson, and it is an animal aberration only in the limited sense of human values. It is a natural reaction to exploitation of habitat and wild prey species and must be compared with the ecological disasters triggered by exploitation in river catchment areas in the guise of flooding, siltation and other attendant catastrophes. Yet, though we cannot retaliate against the stark mountain sides for choking our waterways by siltation, we seek to destroy the politically unprotected tiger who has been compelled by adverse biotic activities to kill a human. Maneaters are generally created by reactionary human activities, and their elimination should not be sought as an automatic

solution to a socio-ecological problem. The devastating floods caused
by the insensate exploitation of timber in catchment areas is an
ecological crisis, but we do not seek to dam the river or alter its course
if it has washed away whole villages and rendered millions destitute
and homeless. We go in for vast afforestation schemes to prevent the
further erosion of our mountain slopes. Yet, though the killing of a
human by a tiger is a similar natural reaction against the encroachment, despoliation of habitat areas and poaching of wild prey species,
we seek not to remedy the situation we have created, but adopt the
simpler and irresponsible solution of destruction because of the
vulnerability of the tiger, who has no vote and no jurisprudence to
support his claim to existence.

The Wildlife (Protection) Act of 1972 in Section I, sub-section II,
clause Ia defines the procedure for dealing with maneaters: 'The Chief
Wildlife Warden may, if he is satisfied that any wild animal specified
in Schedule I has become dangerous to human life—by order in
writing, and stating the reasons thereof, permit any person to hunt
such animal, or cause such an animal to be hunted.' Hunting is
described as capturing, killing, poisoning, snaring and trapping any
wild animal. The operative discretion lies solely with the Chief
Wildlife Warden, and inspite of the qualifying statement of 'stating
the reasons thereof', there is no doubt that he is the final authority,
the Lord High Executioner with the powers of life and death. However, the framers of the Act did not envisage the recurrent phenomena
of maneating caused by habitat degradation by human encroachment
and intrusion, and the onus which devolves on a single bureaucrat,
pressurized by political superiors, needs to be amended. The present
situation would be ludicrous if it were not tragic. A Central Government guideline issued under the aegis of Project Tiger, the Authority
in charge of Policy governing this specialist subject, states categorically that a maneater will not be declared as such until the animal is
confirmed as compulsively seeking human flesh as prey and has
devoured more than one person. Yet, under political pressure tigers
are declared maneaters after one killing, or even mauling, although
they happen to be tigresses with cubs; and they are often slaughtered
by irresponsible people a considerable time after the declaration,
even though no further incident has taken place, and without iden-
tification as to whether the designated animal is the one eliminated.
Moreover, the killing of the tiger is treated as a status operation by
the appointed person, and the State government further compounds
the process of destruction by awarding the trophy to the killer.
Suggestions have also been made that the hunting of maneaters could

be treated as a commercial operation in order to earn foreign exchange—for wildlife must pay for its conservation even in death.

1978 to 1988 were watershed years for the tiger. Tara, the fifth-generation, zoo-bred tigress returned to the wild in the middle of January 1978. Three different human killings took place by an amazing coincidence by three different tigers in March, within a radius of 65 kilometres, and after a lapse of seventeen years. Three tigers had also been involved in 1959–61, when they reacted to an extended colonization of grassland adjoining the Nepal border in order to resettle landless labour from Eastern U.P. in a vote-catching effort by the local government. However, finding the process of reclamation too demanding, these feckless and fecund settlers hit upon a novel method of augmenting their assets. They gathered a quantity of old bones which they brought to the home of the government Colonization Officer, bewailing the fact that a tiger had eaten the bullocks they had bought with the loan given, and demanding further advances. Needless to say, the land broken up by government tractor power started going back to grass, and the situation was only saved by displaced personnel from Punjab who, with the hardihood of people from that region, bought and cultivated the land from the original owners who then continued as indentured and bonded labour. Under such conditions of disrupted habitat, these three tigers were declared maneaters, and regrettably I shot them, not having acquired at the time the maturity of consideration or empathy which I now possess.

Over a period of ten years, beginning with 1978, over two hundred humans were killed by tigers in the district of Kheri, and the human launched a ghastly series of reprisals. Tigers were poisoned and found lying next to domestic stock and surrounded by dead vultures. Decapitated carcasses were discovered on railway tracks, where they had been placed to appear as train accidents. Corpses floated down canals where poisoned animals overcome by a raging thirst collapsed as they drank. They were shot, and electrocuted by stretching live wires along boundaries of forest and field, and crude bombs exploded in their jaws as they fed on their kills of cattle. Alarmed by the number of human casualties, and queried by their political masters, sycophantic officials declared tigers as maneaters on the least pretext, and used this as an excuse to kill any tiger. I list below a few of these futile incidents.

In July 1984 a tigress was declared a maneater outside the Dudhwa

National Park. A tiger was shot over the kill with two canines, his premolars and incisors, blown out by a charge of buckshot. The tigress still remains a declared maneater. In April 1985 a tigress with cubs mauled a man who was attempting to plunder a hogdeer kill. She was declared a maneater. In August the same year a man enticed a woman into a canefield. He killed her thereafter, but it was declared to be the handiwork of a tiger. David Hunt, an ornithologist, was killed by a tiger when he entered the forest in pursuit of an owl. A tigress with cubs was suspected, but the tiger's life was saved when Hunt's sorrowing companions admitted that it was not the tiger's fault.

A cyclist, pedalling past a canefield at the dead of night, fell off in a drunken stupor and was dragged into cover by a tiger. A month later and fifteen miles away, a Research Officer from the Corbett National Park fired at and wounded a tiger, supposedly the maneater, which was found and burnt by the Tiger Watch five miles away. A month later, a tigress was declared to be a maneater, but a male tiger was captured in a baited cage. He was sent to the zoo! The Chief Wildlife Warden issued a blanket order that free-ranging tigers outside Dudhwa National Park should be captured and sent to zoos.

On Christmas Eve, 1988, a tiger was shot in the Kukrail forests, a picnic resort, eight miles from Lucknow. The closest habitat with resident tigers was over 100 miles away, and it is a matter of astonishment as to how a disoriented animal located the only fragmented habitat amidst an unlimited concrete jungle and cultivated fields. Though surrounded by humans in residence, the tiger was able to selectively kill a nilgai from among the scanty wildlife which inhabited the area. The Chief Wildlife Warden, the bureaucrat in charge of wildlife management, had two options. He could have immobilized the tiger and returned him to the closest holding forest, or he could have arranged to have him trapped in a baited cage, as had been done frequently.

However, though this incident took place close to his headquarters, no action was taken to save the life of India's national animal, and two days later a newspaper caption read 'Maneater to be stuffed'. 'It is learnt that the experts who brought an end to the roving tiger will be given suitable cash rewards.'

Such pressures against the survival of the tiger have built up all over the world, and four subspecies are extinct in the wild, and mere holding actions cannot save those which have gone, and it can merely delay the departure of those still extant.

During 1986 and 1987 several dead tigers were recovered. No one knows how many more were killed, and their skins and bones sent to markets in the Far East. In 1985 the skeletons of five tigers were discovered in the possession of two men and one woman. The woman was released, and the two men exonerated by the magistrate as this was their 'first offence'. These bones were apparently on their way to China, where a flourishing market exists and where wine and medicine is made from tiger bones. The South China Tiger is nearly extinct in the wilds, yet it is proposed that the farming of tigers should be started for this purpose. After this harvest we will have no reservoir, and all will be in the shop window.

The crisis in India, particularly in the Dudhwa National Park, has been triggered by the wholesale destruction of habitat in Nepal. Initially, the traditional home of the tiger, and the source of graduated supply to the Indian forests, unbridled felling of timber and reclamation of grasslands caused an unnatural surplus immigration to India, with which the receiving country, burdened as they were with similar problems of habitat destruction, could not cope. In addition, the immigrant tigers found favourable niches already occupied by residents and were obliged to settle for the occupation of ersatz and temporary cover in sugarcane plantations, where wild prey species had been decimated by poachers and illegal hunters supposedly protecting their crops. This laid the scene for conflict between the tiger and the human.

Unfortunately, the artificial surplus which immigrated into India consequent to the destruction of the breeding grounds of the tiger in the sub-montane tract of the Churia Range in Nepal, was treated as an indication of the success of wildlife schemes in India. But now that the surplus had been gleaned owing to the unfortunate, but unavoidable, human/tiger confrontation, the tiger population plummetted sharply in the 1980s. Great care must now be taken while conducting censuses to ensure that we do not reach a point of no return, for unfortunately a complacency due to apparent population increases is manifest in the statements made by the forest officials in charge of wildlife management procedures.

In addition, the linking of Wildlife with Forests as a State subject in the Constitution sealed the fate of wild animals. In the 1970s, the promulgation of an Emergency enabled Mrs Gandhi to put Wildlife on the Concurrent List, which implied in theory that the Central Government was empowered to legislate on policy concerned with Wildlife. In practise, however, the State of Uttar Pradesh, which is the largest in India, holds the key to power at the Centre. The Central Government thus has to be extremely circumspect on matters concerning the State, which is extremely touchy regarding so-called interference. Basically, the States are anti-wildlife as the electorate suffer from the depredations of wild animals. They are willing to pay lip service to the concept of conservation because of international pressures, but the ultimate onus of administration falls on them, and any guidelines by the Centre are ignored in the supposed interest of the voting public. Without attempting to be discursive, I shall give a pertinent example of the functioning of the key Department holding charge for the conservation of our national animal, the tiger.

Seeing the situation develop, the Directorate of Wildlife of the Central Government have objectively made certain suggestions to be followed before the declaration of a maneater. The State in total disregard for these guidelines brings pressure to bear on the sole bureaucrat responsible for the declaration of a maneater. As confrontations developed and local feelings became exacerbated, the Chairman of the Indian Wildlife Board visited the Dudhwa National Park. He was waited upon by various delegations, including one of the local Bus Owners Union, who expressed great concern for the travelling public who, they claimed, were inhibited by lurking maneating tigers from catching connecting buses. Needless to say, the bus owners were more concerned with the fares they thought they were losing. They blamed Tara, and her supposed inability to subdue wild prey, as being largely responsible for these enforced killings. An enquiry committee was therefore appointed with a senior Field Director of Project Tiger as the principal investigator. He was given a mandate for carrying out a survey of the maneating situation in the Dudhwa National Park and its environs. As he happened to be rearing a young tigress who alternated between living in a caged enclosure in his custody with occasional visits to the Simlipal Tiger Reserve in Orissa, he also thought fit to pass strictures on Tara, who by that time was passing through a transition period in her return to life as a wild tigress.

While admitting that habitat had been degraded and prey species decimated, in a verbose and confused statement he made the astonishing claim that due to the androus presence of the tiger in a restricted habitat the population was increasing, 'contrary to Malthusian principles'. In addition, he made the most regressive recommendations that, if in the haste to destroy a so-called maneater, the wrong tiger was destroyed, it did not matter; that poison was permissible to ensure speedy killing; and that the utility of tigers could be revived as a commercial resource. Regarding my hand reared tigress, he made the ignorant statement that she had been eliminated and not naturally rehabilitated; and he gratuitously observed that it was impossible to reintroduce super-predators. This remark was obviously triggered by the fact that he had also been raising a tigress who had become so imprinted by the administration of artificial restraints that she had become overweight and was not interested in males; it was now claimed that she was never intended to be rehabilitated in nature. My tigress, who had been reared normally, was uncontrollable in her desire to return to her kind. I therefore concluded that the report was an adverse reaction to my claim that a zoo-bred tigress had been introduced to free living conditions, which did not appeal to the forester who had inflicted the final indignity of bondage on a free animal. It was a very unhappy viewpoint for people who had been entrusted with an international mandate to save a species from extinction to uphold. The final remark of the report was that 'no super-predator can be rehabilitated that way'—which illustrates the official view of maintaining the status quo, a the gradual process of attrition which can only lead to extinction.

The International Union for the Conservation of Nature and Natural Resources, the international body which deals with the propagation of natural species, recommends a contiguous population of 300 tigers to maintain a viable gene pool in perpetuity, which would require an area of about 2,000 to 3,000 square miles. Though it is possible that wild animals can withstand more in breeding than domestic stock, such large areas are not available anywhere in India. Therefore, the only answer is the ad hoc turnover of a gene pool to maintain a viability, and this can only be accomplished by fresh introductions, in three ways.

Hand reared animals may be reintroduced. Such a process will require dedicated and expert handling and is an operation that lasts a year and a half to two years; I am the only man to have done it with a tiger. Secondly, immobilized animals from different localities may be interchanged. Such an operation will probably have to be confined to tigresses who are generally more tolerant than male conspecifics, who have a greater sense of territoriality and may object to the intrusion of a foreign male—though tigers inhabiting areas well stocked with prey can coexist if not overcrowded. However, in cases of conspecific aggression it is better if one tiger is killed in a range intrusion, which is their form of population control, than that an entire genus should be branded for man-slaughter. Lastly, there remains the media of artificial insemination, which is a complicated biological process requiring considerable technical know how.

The priorities of wildlife conservation have inevitably got mixed up, for though it is essentially an international subject, wildlife has no visas. Yet, since the world is governed by humans, national constraints have to be accepted as being essential for administration: migratory birds pass through many countries, and India cannot do anything to stop the slaughter of Siberian Cranes in Pakistan. A tigress was found with her head shattered as someone had placed a bomb in her kill, but no inquiry was possible as she had come from Nepal and died in India. Developed countries have collected a great deal of money to save the tiger, but we claim Project Tiger as a totally Indian concern, and resented a mid-term appraisal carried out by an internationally appointed Commission. But we have given over the Project's administration to the politically pressurized States. Though the project is in the central sector, the Government of India has unilaterally committed the States to sharing half the expenditure in the hope of motivating them, and releases funds only when the State has produced its share. The latter claim that their budget is not enough for human needs, and as a result allotted funds become time barred and have to be refunded unspent to the Revenue Department.

In a democracy, wildlife cannot exist without the support of the people. Unless people living on the periphery benefit from the wildlife area and are proud of it, that area cannot remain. In India, if a tiger kills the draught animal of one of the peripheral inhabitants, he is either paid no compensation or it is very tardily awarded with a cut for corrupt officials, as the Central Government has unilaterally committed the States for payment, and they claim to have no funds for such payment. As a result, there is great resentment against conservation and tigers are poisoned in reprisal. The same applies to depredations by other animals. The voter becomes automatically allied to the anti-wildlife lobby. The situation is a particularly anomalous one, for the peripheral dwellers see no reason to pander to the exhortations by government forums, influenced by international bodies, to save wildlife, when their very existence is threatened. It is fortunate that the animism of the Hindu pantheon of gods generally militates against blood sports; but the invidious destruction, without violence, of habitat degradation is exceedingly subtle in its impact, and therefore more lethal in its final consummation. Unless it is possible to excise particular areas for wildlife, and allow them to remain inviolate, it is not possible for competitors to coexist with the master predator, for unlike the one who savoured the Lady of Riga, the tiger now has nothing to smile about, with his living space increasingly encroached upon.

The Forest Department is a commercial organization, yet it has charge of wildlife because of administrative convenience, and it resists the expansion of wildlife areas as the Wildlife Act lays down that such areas will not be exposed to commercial exploitation. These are small islands of conservation under siege from the human invader. The result is that tiger areas are too small to retain a genetic diversity, and inspite of a temporary increase in numbers, tigers will perforce suffer from the effects of inbreeding at a later stage. The great cats are essentially territorial animals, and though a good deal of tolerance is possible among young tigers when there is plenty of prey available, together with a familial relationship, there are limits beyond which populations cannot increase in a given spatial area. Thereafter numbers become self adjusting, either by animals moving into buffer areas, if available; through conspecific competition, or possible restriction of breeding due to stresses of overcrowding. It is, therefore, inevitable that small populations will run the risk of deterioration, and every effort should be made to increase the area of Reserves, even at the expense of cutting down on some smaller and less viable wilderness areas. Finally, such single-minded management can only be carried out effectively by a separate Wildlife Service. The Forest Department, apart from other preoccupations with the environment, is too diversified to effectively look after a 'non-subject' like wildlife.

In an underdeveloped country where the majority of people live below the subsistence level, the conservation of wildlife is an aesthetic subject initiated by international influence, and therefore should be apolitical, and controlled by a Directing Authority. It is also obvious that a State government cannot look after it, what with its political motivations and commitments. Moreover, thanks to human occupation, the expansion of tiger populations must be contained by constriction of available habitat, after which they will adjust their own populations.

However, as I have often pointed out, the maneating problem has been aggravated by the plantation of an ersatz but seasonal habitat crop in the guise of sugarcane, which has enabled a population expansion; but with available prey populations of wild ungulates having been decimated by crop protection weaponry, tigers have come to depend on domestic stock and, eventually, human prey. It should also be realized that vast areas of grassland were claimed for agriculture and the displaced tigers, which could not be accommodated in adjoining forest areas, remained in these cane areas in a temporary habitat. An additional and massive immigration took place with an influx of tigers from Nepal, when they were displaced from their ancestral homes in the Tarai of the Churia or Shivalik Range by the unbridled felling of trees by the new rulers of Nepal.

It is tragic for me that, at the end of my life, I have fought a a battle which can only end in defeat; yet I must soldier on. If I abandon the cause, I could never life with myself. Starting as a compulsive killer, I have run the entire gamut: conscientious evaluator to conservationist, preservationist, and, ultimately, crusader. I have the satisfying feeling that, inspite of eventual failure, tempered in nature's crucible, I am a more civilized person than when I began.

But one must realize that society and social living is in itself conducive to aberrant behaviour, due to our competitive existences; and the world with its mounting population, growing away from natural controls, is an invitation to increasingly traumatic conditions of social existence. We need to compare the life-style of the solitary tiger to that of the social lion to appreciate the behavioural differences between individuals and communities. Tigers will sit around and wait their turn, and adults seldom feed together. Their faces are unmarked and unblemished. Lions squabble and jostle to get to the kill, and the weakest starve. Their scarred visages are a reflection of the wounded human psyche in the trauma of competitive existence.

In November 1969 the General Assembly of the International Union for Nature and Natural Resources met in New Delhi. K.S. Sankhala presented a forceful paper on the deteriorating status of the tiger, and I tabled a Resolution suggesting a moratorium on tiger shooting. By a unanimous verdict, the tiger was put on to the Red Data Book, and the Assembly resolved that the hunting of tigers should be replaced by their tourist potential. The Secretary of the Smithsonian Institution also undertook to initiate a Project for a census of the tiger population which had fallen to a low of 1,827.

The next year Guy Mountfort, a Trustee of the WWF, the funding body of the IUCN, came to India and offered Mrs Gandhi, the then Prime Minister of India, a million dollars towards a Project for the conservation of the tiger. She reacted with characteristic alacrity and a Task Force was appointed under whose recommendation Project Tiger was inaugurated at the Corbett National Park in 1973, initially with nine Project Areas. A tremendous euphoria prevailed, and my

1 Raja Sir Harman Singh,
the author's grandfather

2 Jasbir Singh,
the author's father

3 The author (standing)
and his older brother,
Jaswant; c. 1920

4 The author with his first tiger

5   Balrampur group; the author's father is seated in the centre of the first row of chairs

6 *Maharaja Joodha Shumshere Jung of Nepal, with only some of his tiger skins*

7 *Human revenge: decapitated carcass found near a railway track*

8 *The father shares a meal with his cubs*

9–10   *Tigress charging at an interloper; two cubs are in the background*

11 Glowing eyes
reflected in flashlight
photographs—proof
of their patience

12 Long Toes

13 *The Median Tigress, dead*

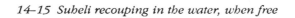

14–15 *Suheli recouping in the water, when free*

15 Suheli recouping in the water, when free

16 Suheli in the Delhi zoo

17 The Maneater of Salukapur, alive

18 The Maneater of Salukapur, dead

19 *The wounded Male Cub*

20 *Splay Toes, with an angling gash across his nose*

21 *Splay Toes, snarling with mouth agape, devoid of canines*

22 *Abubakr, in the company of a buffalo*

23 Captive monarch: Sheroo in the Kanpur zoo

24 Tara's Male sharing the water with his son

25 Tara's third set of cubs
26 Tara pouncing

27 Tara's mate for the first three matings

*28 Tara's mate
for the fourth mating*

29 *Tara, with blood on mouth*

30 *The last photograph taken of Tara*

31 *A broken Splay Toes, scowling at alighting vultures*

32 Tiger, leopard and dog in peaceful co-existence

suggestion at a meeting of the Indian Board for Wildlife that the tiger should replace the lion as our national animal, was accepted. Unfortunately, Sankhala, who had been appointed as Director of the Project, and the Inspector General of Forests, opposed the import of telemetric equipment, and the Smithsonian census and study scheme went by default to Nepal. But the tiger took its place at the biotic apex of the ecosystem, and became a symbol for the protection of the entire forest complex over which he held sway. The initial desire to make the project a success was great, and under its impetus and the stoppage of commercial operations, the status of the tiger greatly improved. But unfortunately census figures became a status symbol for Field Directors who conducted their own counts, and became enmeshed in the web of the numbers game—the figures have been impossibly exaggerated, from where there is no official return.

However, the unfortunate aspect has been the change of attitude of the bureaucracy supervising the Project, pressurized as it is by the attitudes of State politicians. Influenced by the so-called maneating phenomena, the emphasis is now on 'saving the ecosystem'. The symbol has been displaced and the spectacular tiger is no more the warhead who vitalizes the conservation of the entire ecosystem. Ostensibly, we have intellectually rationalized the concept: but when we abolish godhead, religion is a semantic exercise. Project Tiger has indeed changed direction.

It is a saddening thought that the protection of the environment is assuming a greater significance than wildlife. That is perhaps as it must be when man's existence is the prior consideration. For wildlife is part of the environment and, theoretically, if the forests are intact, wildlife should be all right. Of course, this is not so; poaching, sport killing and habitat destruction can erase wildlife and, whereas forests can be replaced, wildlife is gone forever. The other fact is the utility of forests in the control of climate, erosion, flooding and xerification, and the direct impact, and unforeseen influences, they may have on human survival. The existence of wildlife under such conditions is incidental, and the only usage they have is their importance as indicators for the benefit of the human race. There is, therefore, the great danger of the subject of wildlife conservation being consigned to the sidelines under the influence of the growing panic concerning natural retaliations against the excesses we have imposed on the environment.

The Dudhwa National Park was declared as such under the aegis of the Emergency on 1 February 1977. The proposal had been sponsored by Mrs Indira Gandhi, to whom the wildlife concept owes such a great deal. She had written to the Chief Minister of U.P. suggesting the declaration of Dudhwa as a Park, chiefly because of my personal affiliation and dedication to the ideals of conservation. She wrote on 31 December 1973: 'I hope you will give every encouragement to Arjan Singh also. He has ploughed a lonely furrow for many years. It is easy to come by arm-chair conservationists, but rare indeed to find a man with the dedication and perseverance to act in support of a cause which he loves.' Eighteen years later the Park lives on, surrounded by an increasing human population who eventually must overwhelm the wilderness, and those who stand in the way.

There was great opposition to the declaration of the Park by the Forest Department. The quality of timber was the finest in India, and it was felt that the sacrifice of revenue for the creation of a wildlife refuge was neither practical nor financially viable. But Mrs Gandhi was insistent. Her government fell due to a harsh implementation of Family Planning, but the Park had been declared as such, and though the succeeding government tried to gather enough support to de-recognize the Park, and though the Chief Minister slashed the wildlife budget with the remark that a poor state could not afford luxuries, Mrs Gandhi in the Opposition managed to delay legislation until the new government fell and she was once more back in the saddle. Wildlife, which had been placed on the Concurrent List during the Emergency was sought to be returned to State legislation; but this was foiled once again by Mrs Gandhi.

The watershed year of 1978 for the tiger is also one for the tormented Dudhwa National Park. The Park's Committee, consisting of senior government officials, was formed in 1976, and my interest in the Park was recognized when I was nominated as a member. One of the first resolutions was the proposal for the establishment of a project on the boundary river of the Soheli which runs past my residence at Tiger Haven. On my firm opposition, the Chairman agreed to categorically negate the proposal of a barrage, as its construction would be harmful to the swampdeer, which was listed in the IUCN Red Data Book as an endangered species, and for whom the Park had been specifically designated. The Secretary of the Irrigation Department, however, bided his time in a typical governmental subterfuge, and awaited the superannuation of the Chairman. He then began a clandestine construction of the barrage, and when questioned at a meeting of the Committee declared his ignorance of the fact that the construction was in the buffer zone of the Park. He was able to persuade the new Chairman of his bona fides, and blackmailed him into getting approval, because a great deal of Departmental funds had been spent. The Chairman cleared the project inspite of my opposition, and the result has been that the closure of the barrage gates at flood level has raised the flood level by over two metres at Tiger Haven, which is on the river; and it has drowned swampdeer fawns which are dropped in May to July. The population has, as a result, fallen dramatically. Water-logging has also degraded the habitat.

1978, has another significance. It was triggered in the Park by the proposal that wind-fallen timber should be extracted in a limited operation. The proposal had distinctly commercial overtones and was mainly because the Forest Department wished to retain its commercial nexus with the Park. As such an operation was forbidden under the Wildlife Act, I opposed its implementation at a meeting of the Dudhwa National Park Committee. However, the Chairman guaranteed a proposal whereby the sale proceeds would be credited to Park funds. The Finance Secretary, who was present, did not demur, and I had willy nilly to agree to an attractive proposition, which I later discovered was ultra vires of Government procedures. A prolonged logging process was initiated, entailing considerable disturbance to prime tiger habitat. The operation only ceased when a tiger killed a cartman and his bullock in a typical ecological reaction to this Departmental invasion. The sale proceeds amounted to Rs 32,00,000, but the Finance Department, who had originally agreed to the allocation proposal, refused to release the funds to the Park budget. There is a Section 420 under the Indian Penal Code which prescribes severe penalties for fraud, but the government appears to be immune to its application.

Opposition was also built up against me in my efforts to introduce a young tigress into the National Park. Such an experiment had the approval of the Prime Minister, but as a young tigress had not been available in India, this tigress had to be brought from Twycross Zoo in England, which the Forest Department claimed would defile the purity of the Indian race as she was from a different subspecies. Moreover, the Department refused to permit a radio collaring at the time of release, and then claimed that Tara had been destroyed as a maneater nearly three years after she went wild. The maneating phenomena which was caused by tigers finding breeding cover in sugarcane crops, grown recklessly on the border of the Park from where prey animals had been shot by agriculturists, was blamed on Tara who, according to the so-called pundits, had not learnt the art of hunting. But I claim that predators do not need to be taught, for instinctive knowledge is passed on through their genes. A massive hatred was built up against the tiger, an animal that in earlier years the cultivator had claimed to be their unpaid watchman as no grazing ungulate trespassed when the great cat passed through the field.

Consequent to the visit from the Union Finance Minister and the Chairman of the Indian Board for Wildlife in 1978, a committee had been formed to assess the maneating problem in the district. Among other recommendations was the suggestion that a 'Tiger Watch' should be formed to monitor the activities of suspect tigers. Six years later, this organization has become a phantom, its budget curtailed by the Finance Department, and its conveyance cannibalized by higher authority. My offer of participation was refused, and the Watch remains a moribund institution shunned by all forest officers as an unrewarding administrative posting.

Soon after, I shot or assisted in destroying three so-called maneating tigers at the request of the various Directors of the Park, in 1980–1, 1983–4 and 1984–5. During this period I was also requested by the Forest Department to submit a memorandum to the Fourth Pay Commission recommending an increase in their emoluments, and also to signify my willingness to testify before the Commission if called upon to do so.

Meanwhile, the first Director of the Park, who had been there for a period of six years, managed to get himself posted back for another two years. He recommended to the government that concessions hitherto allowed to villagers within a five-kilometre limit on a quid pro quo basis, should now be allowed to all comers in order to earn the goodwill of the local population who had been upset by the declaration of the area as a Park which disallowed any commercial operation within its confines. No orders could be issued by the government ultra vires of the Wildlife Act, but the Director started implementing these measures for all comers who, by payment of Rs 100 per bullock cart, instead of the official rate of Rs 25, got their names entered on the list submitted by the concessionist village to the Park Authority. The surplus money was then divided on a pro rata system between the forest staff and the village headman.

Thousands of carts were let loose in the Park, and they plundered fuel wood and timber and sold it in the Palia market. A tiger killed four of these intruders in defence of his habitat, but the Director reacted by cancelling the celebration of Park Day. I went to the extent of pointing out that Republic Day was not cancelled because a Prime Minister had been assassinated, but he was playing well and truly to the political gallery. Ironically, I was obliged to destroy this tiger, as, encouraged by those four human killings, it next killed the Range Officer in charge of the Rhino Reintroduction Project; he was returning home in the late evening on a motorcycle, as the Director had commandeered the motor vehicle belonging to the Project.

An honest Director who was posted to the Park in 1986 and attempted to control the looting of the Park was complained against by the local Legislative Assembly member. Subsequently, the Chief Secretary came to make an enquiry, and a public delegation praised the previous Director for his public relations, and blamed the present incumbent and me for causing hardship to the people. I remarked to the Chief Secretary that, if this robbery went on, the Park would be sold in the local market within five years. Thereafter, the Chief Minister arrived and issued verbal orders that concessions should continue as previously. I thereupon applied for a stay from the High Court, thereby earning a respite for the Park habitat, but incurring the enmity of the politician and the Department. The Chief Minister retaliated and bifurcated the portfolios of Forests and Wildlife and, while allocating Forests to another minister added Wildlife to the sixty portfolios he allegedly handled. The present Director was summarily transferred, and an officer two ranks junior, and with a dubious record of service, was appointed.

Soon after, a tiger killed a man on the Palia-Dudhwa Road. He created a reign of terror along the highway. I reported the matter to the Director and Tiger Watch. As the authorities took no action, and the tiger had taken to visiting Tiger Haven and become a threat to my staff, I baited the tiger in the Park and discovered that he had lost his canines. I reported the matter to the Director, but instead of taking effective measures against the tiger, he took action against me. He raided the site where I had baited, confiscated the equipment I had used to discover the cause of the tiger's infirmity, and filed a criminal case against me for baiting to make commercial films and attract foreign tourists.

It is my contention that a pliable Director was posted by the Chief Minister to stop me from preventing the plunder of the Park, and the loss of franchise due to the exclusion of the public from the Park. The situation is even more ironic as I had continually suggested at meetings of the Indian Board for Wildlife, that permanent residences, and cooking facilities should be granted to peripheral inhabitants of wildlife areas in order to earn their goodwill and prevent their intrusion into the Park. Yet the government continues to encourage these dwellers to rely on perishable material from inside the forest.

Wildlife cannot pay for its own protection by the degradation of the habitat, for its seems that the bell has tolled both for wildlife and for the endangered species who strive to protect them.

The tiger is the cynosure of every wildlife tourist's questing eye, among the best known animals in the world, renowned for its matchless beauty and grace, accepted by industry as the ultimate in power advertisement, a symbol of mystery in folklore and legend, and a divinity to primitive people. But the sands are running out for the tiger. Thoughtful and caring persons must pose the question: *Quo Vadis Panthera Tigris*?

As I gaze into the crystal bowl, I see green mountain sides, refulgent in the freshness of their replanted slopes. I see river valleys, the lush forests of catchment areas, and the limpid waters as they commence their unending journey to the meeting with the oceans. But no dolphins frolic in the great waterways, and no marsh crocodiles and gharials bask on the sandbanks. No longer are the tall riverine grasses and tamarisk beaten and agitated when they resound to the thunder of a thousand hoofbeats of the galloping swampdeer as they churn the shallow waters into a rainbow mist in the chill winter dawn. Nor do the marshes echo to the shrill screams of the hinds, orchestrated with the deep booming bass of the big antlered stags in homage, as the mighty predator passes. I do not hear the ethereal resonance of the tiger's call as it re-echoes in the forest canopy, or the sawing grunts of the leopard as he returns to his daytime lair. The stentorian bugling of the barasingha, the piping hunting whistle of the wild dog pack, and the eerie midnight chorus of the jackals are mute, and the chattering bark of the fox no longer consoles the small hours when witches and poltergeists are about. The staccato alarm bark of the muntjac or the metallic trumpet of the sambhar will never shatter the silence of the night, for the King is dead. We are monarchs of all we survey.

6 Quo Vadis –
the Makanpur Maneater

THE Revenue circle of Makanpur is roughly in the form of a triangle. Tiger Haven is situated at the apex of this triangle which points to the north, and is formed by the meeting of the waters of the Soheli and the Neora. From here the Soheli runs due east, forming the northern boundary whereas the tributary Soheli is the western limit. This stream is formed by the backflow of the Neora during the monsoon which fills all the depressions lying in its catchment area. After the rains have ceased the waters from these depressions empty into the source of their origin, and become a mere trickle by the time the succeeding monsoon activates the reverse flow once again. By an administrative quirk, the Soheli after the confluence bequeaths its water as well as its name to the parent Neora. Another small stream known as the Ghulli performs a similar function further downstream, and becomes the eastern and southern boundary. Within this triangle are numerous small farms. Subject to floods, the settlers here lead a precarious existence where they are in competition with crop-grazing ungulates, and tigers into whose domain they have trespassed.

I had very recently acquired the land on which I was to build my living tenements at the confluence; but beyond one small hut, where I used to come and spend a few days, there was no accommodation. I therefore lived at Jasbirnagar, which was the land I had taken on lease immediately after World War II. During one of these visits in 1959 a tiger had taken to killing cattle, and was operating from the grasslands adjoining the North Kheri forests, as they were known before the Dudhwa National Park was declared. As these events took place before the ban on tiger shooting was imposed, it was customary for farmers to shoot the deer which grazed their crops, and the predators which preyed upon their domestic stock. These crop-protectionists were mainly armed with unlicenced ·12 gauge smooth bore guns, and hesitated to try conclusions with the tiger, though accidents did take place, chiefly as a result of mistaken identity. The compulsive destruction of prey species was the direct cause of confrontation between tigers and humans.

Before the monsoon rains a tigress had given birth to cubs in a patch of sugarcane belonging to a local Sikh farmer, and killed his cow. Determined on revenge, he sat on a tree next to his dead cow, and blazed off a charge of buckshot at a pair of lambent eyes, reflected in the light which he shone. The animal bounded off, but no effort was made to follow her. Killings now ceased for a while, and no further trace was found of the tigress or the cubs. The floods were heavy during 1960, and one night when the waters had inundated all the land in the Makanpur triangle, a tigress broke into some hutments outside of the southern tip of the triangle, and killed another cow. It was surmised that the heavy flooding had restricted her movements, and that she had been compelled to make this daring assault on the property of her human neighbours. Alarmed by the hullabaloo, she abandoned the kill to which she did not return.

Her next kill was a human whom she killed in a shallow reed bed, but as frequently happens in the case of a first human kill, a tiger will eat the genitals, and then abandon the carcass, for it appears that in the case of the human the body contour is unfamiliar, and tigers are puzzled as to where to begin. This inhibition probably applies to the first kill, which is frequently accidental. A deliberate killing, impelled by hunger, however, is sufficient inducement for feeding. Thereafter, depending on the degree of compulsion, familiarity breeds contempt and man is included in the prey species available. Soon several human kills took place over a wide area, and the tigress, which after a convalescence had returned to her original range, was declared a maneater. Equally obviously, she had lost her cubs due to her disability, and was once again on her own.

The next attempted kill took place in a sugarcane field in early winter when the tigress pounced on a man while he was stripping cane. She started dragging him into cover, but luckily for him, other strippers hearing his screams while he was clamped in the jaws of his attacker, ran to this rescue, and set off in pursuit banging tin cans and shouting. In the end the tigress dropped the man who had lacerated wounds on his head and neck. He was taken to the local hospital where he recovered after prolonged treatment. He is still alive, and probably one of the very few people who have been recovered alive from a purposeful attack by a tiger.

The tigress' last victim was a woman named Kailasia. Of doubtful sanity, origin and virtue, she spent her time grazing other people's cattle, for which she was paid by the head. One afternoon she had taken the cattle to the edge of a marsh to feed, when some graziers nearby suddenly heard a single scream, and Kailasia's herd stampeded across the meadow. This incident took place within half a mile of Tiger Haven and I went to investigate.

A khair tree (*Acacia catechu*) stood on the edge of the swamp, charred by burning, and bleached white by the droppings of innumerable birds over the years. The only sign of death was an expectant, solitary vulture perched on the burnt stump. As I climbed the tree the vulture flapped heavily away, but there was nothing to be seen. Next I searched the immediate area and came across a primitive fishing rod, and a small rush basket of mud fish by a pool of water on the edge of the marsh. A few drops of blood and the pugmarks of a tigress in the damp earth showed where Kailasia had been surprised. By this time the evening was closing in, and I decided that further action would have to be delayed, since the trail led into dense and tall grass.

Next morning I returned with my elephant Bhagwan Piari, and found the tigress feeding on the dead body not far from where I had found the fishing rod. On my approach, she retreated into some reeds, two acres in extent and surrounded by scorched grass which had just been burnt. The reeds were too wet to be burnt, so I stalked the tigress from one clump to the other. Now and then I caught a glimpse of the tigress as she tried to hide behind the reeds. Despite her formidable reputation, she looked quite small and helpless.

However, I did not wish to risk a long shot with the light rifle I was carrying, for the tigress might suddenly take off across the burnt grass and escape, since by now she appeared to have little fear of humans. I followed the tigress carefully, waiting for the chance of a good shot. Soon she appeared out of a patch of reeds, and stood broadside to me as I fired. As the crack of cordite echoed across the marsh, she gave one convulsive leap, and collapsed.

She was a young tigress with a beautiful coat, and a broken jaw. The bone had calloused over where the jaw had been shot away. Her right canine was broken at the root, and there was a large hole in the palate. A suppurating wound at the back of the head, which indicated another ill-conceived and later shot, was full of maggots. It was a sorry sight, and remarkable that she had survived for over a year in that condition; and hardly surprising that she had taken to maneating.

7 *The Maneaters of Tirkolia and Visenpuri*

THE holocaust of Partition in 1947 triggered a fresh demand for agricultural land with the influx of displaced personnel from the Punjab. Powerful tractors cleared vast areas of forest, originally in the district of Naini Tal, and then moved to the adjoining districts of Pilibhit and Kheri. Soon settlers from the Punjab started moving in, and the wilderness to which I had originally arrived as a pioneer settler was cleared for cultivation. Many of the settlers from the hot and dry climate of their origin succumbed to the damp and malarious surroundings they had immigrated to, but the families stayed on, and soon the sturdy husbandmen integrated, and have become a part of the land to which they now belong. So thoroughly have the Sikh farmers taken over agriculture in this part of U.P. that some politicians who claim Khalistan as a homeland for the Sikhs include the tarai areas of Naini Tal, Pilibhit and Kheri in it.

Visenpuri is a settlement ten miles to the west of Tiger Haven. In 1959 the original government concept of confiscating large agricultural landholdings and distributing them among landless labour from Eastern U.P. was just getting under way. Agricultural machinery, and important officials arrived in force, but despite generous handouts, and a great deal of talk, no one seemed to be able to arouse much interest for the scheme among the settlers who were supposed to be its beneficiaries. This set of settlers came from a region where people prefer not to work if they can avoid it. Finding the local conditions for agriculture unattractive, they looked around for less demanding ways of earning a living. We have already noted in a previous chapter that many sold the pair of bullocks they had been given, and then went into the marshes and collected a pile of old bones and skeletons, loudly proclaiming that the cattle had been devoured by tigers. This ploy put them in line for a claim for compensation, and also gave an excuse for branding the tiger a cattle lifter, and therefore to be shot. Government officials were only too ready to cooperate with these schemes, since they could be worked out to the mutual advantage of all concerned. Someone would arrange for a colleague to declare a cattle lifter, and then go and shoot it himself, perhaps collecting in due course the reward which had been placed on the tiger's head. Thus bounties were proclaimed and rewards claimed, and it became quite a popular pastime for senior officials to combine business with pleasure. All they needed was a suitable pretext, and the presence of a so-called maneater of course.

It was therefore with considerable caution that I listened to the story related by the Colonization Officer and various local landlords, who drew up one morning in a large truck. They told me with great seriousness that the entire resettlement scheme was in jeopardy because a maneating tiger had arrived in the area. The day before, apparently, a small boy who had been cutting grass near his field, had been killed and partly eaten. The Colonization Officer insisted that though this was the first casualty, others were bound to follow. Already the settlers were so scared that they talked of abandoning their holdings. Though the reasoning was obscure, they asked persuasively whether I would come to their rescue and kill the maneater.

I had acquired a reputation for an affinity with the forests and for following up wounded tigers, which was why they had come to me for assistance. I knew that the Colonization Authorities had been issued with a ·375 Magnum rifle for just such a situation and should normally be only too delighted to carry out this task of trophy and reward hunting. So I asked the Colonization Officer why he did not deal with the tiger on his own. He then admitted to never having fired a rifle in his life. He claimed that he was more at home with a shotgun and buckshot, which he used regularly for spotlight shooting from his jeep. He was particularly adept at firing off at random at deer, killing some in the process and wounding others.

I agreed to go to the site of the killing, and a few hours later came upon the tracks of a large male tiger. The story was that the tiger had killed the boy and then eaten one of his legs, but it was impossible to confirm this as the boy had already been buried. I remained sceptical. It seemed to me quite possible that the boy had been killed, since accidents often occur in sugarcane fields if a tiger is suddenly disturbed. But that he should have been eaten seemed less likely. Short of exhuming the body, however, there was nothing to be done, and I was committed to an adventure which I felt from the beginning might easily have been a mistake.

The first thing I did was to instruct the official to tie up buffalo bait for the tiger, and a month later I received a message that one of the baits had been killed. It was a cold and cloudy February day, and by noon it had started to drizzle. I had arranged to go to Visenpuri in the afternoon, since tigers are quite likely to visit their kills in daylight during cloudy weather. When I arrived at the location at two o'clock I found an elephant ready to take me to the scene. My initial plan was to climb from the animal's back on to the overlooking machan. But when I was told the machan had a ladder, I decided to dispense with the elephant to minimize disturbance.

However, the ladder, though most artistically constructed, was made of rope and swayed alarmingly. It was while I was swaying to and fro in the manner of a trapeze artist that the tiger arrived to investigate and began to growl. Though perfectly safe at the height I had reached, it was a rather frustrating and undignified performance, since I was unable to get any higher. Nor was the prospect for swaying indefinitely above an expectant maneater particularly appealing. I therefore hastily descended, recovered the elephant and mounted the machan from its back. The time was now three o'clock, and from my vantage point in the tree I could see the head and rib-cage of the buffalo, which is all that remained of the animal. It appeared a great deal for even a large tiger to eat at one sitting.

Time passed slowly, and it continued to drizzle, but as I knew that the tiger was close by I still hoped he would come before darkness fell. At four-thirty two crows dropped down on the carcass, but soon flew up to circle the area towards which the tiger had retreated. He was on the move, and at five o'clock a large, handsome animal appeared, and sat down behind a scanty bush about a hundred yards away. He kept looking back towards the direction from which he had come, and soon a smaller and lither replica of himself, and just as extravagantly marked, came into the open—a tigress.

Her sinuous body caressed him in the manner of a domestic cat, and I could hear the vibrant thrust of her breath through partially closed lips, as she rubbed her head against his. After a few minutes the tiger advanced towards my tree, to see if it was safe to move on towards the kill. He never heard the shot which killed him as he slowly crumpled to the ground. He measured nine feet five inches between pegs. A fine male in unblemished condition. There was no obvious reason why he should have become a maneater; I am convinced that the killing was accidental, and that a life had been taken for a life, as will happen when field encroaches upon forest. Next day I went to see the Colonization Officer. It was bitterly cold and he sat in front of a brazier chewing pan. He kept expertly squirting its red juice into convenient spittoons and remarked that he managed to get through two hundred pans a day. He thanked me profusely for my help, and when I expressed my misgivings, he remarked that democracy in the shape of land distribution had to go on whatever the cost.

The tigress called pathetically that night, and for a long while after that, but a price was on her head also, and she had dwindled to skin and bone by the time she was shot in April for associating with a tiger who had dared to kill a human! Another reward was duly claimed, and the cycle of killing continued. As for the resettlement scheme, many of the original participants abandoned their holdings to become petty thieves and robbers. However, with a leavening of sturdy immigrants from the Punjab who bought over the land from the feckless colonists from Eastern U P., the programme eventually prospered.

Soon after I had shot the so-called maneater at Visenpuri, a tiger of extraordinary boldness appeared near the village of Tirkolia, three miles from my original farm at Jasbirnagar and about fifteen miles from Tiger Haven. It would enter cattle sheds at night and drag away the domestic animals into the tall grass which awaited reclamation. The irate owner used to burn whatever cover he could in the vicinity, often disturbing the tiger at his meal, so killings were much more frequent than had it had been allowed to consume the whole carcass.

In time the tiger claimed its first human victim, an Amli Sikh—one who breaks the Sikh rule forbidding smoking. (In fact, they smoke tobacco and opium, and drink opiates and alcohol in a catholic promiscuity.) He had gone to answer the call of nature in a sugarcane field. As there were large cane plantations in the area, and the man was an itinerant whose wanderings were governed by access to intoxicants, no one really noted his disappearance, except his current employer. The tiger soon lost most of its reluctance to prey on humans, and continued to take an occasional toll from nearby villagers. Usually it was dispossessed of the carcass by yelling Sikhs, who wished to cremate the body according to the rules of their religion, so it became difficult to keep a tag on its movements.

The last but one victim was called Bhaillu, who belonged to one of the lower Hindu sub-castes. Bhaillu lived on a small holding with his wife and two children, and supplemented his income by working as a daily labourer. One night he crept silently out of his house towards a neighbour's threshing floor to steal a pile of winnowed rice which was lying outside waiting to be stored. It was while he was engaged in this act of larceny that the tiger crept up and killed him, and dragged his body into a nearby sugarcane field.

I was immediately informed and set off for the site of the kill. When I arrived there no one had followed up the blood trail, because the sugarcane was extremely dense, but I soon picked up the splayed pugmarks of a large tigress in an adjoining ploughed field. Following the trail was not a pleasant task, as the sugarcane had knife-edge leaves, and it was impossible to see what lay ahead. Nor would I have heard anything if the tigress had attacked, because the crackling of dried leaves underfoot would have drowned the sound of her movements. Eventually I found the body near a khair tree. It was a gruesome sight. The tigress had eaten one leg, and Bhaillu lay stripped of all dignity. One arm, stiff in the rigor of death, pointed accusingly to the heavens. A look of terror distorted his face. I persuaded his relations to leave the body where it was in the hope that the tigress would return, and I then organized a primitive bed for myself, and prepared to spend the night in a machan in the khair tree.

It was an eerie vigil sitting there in the dusk, and in the light of the quartering moon the accusing finger seemed to point me out as the next victim. A jackal repeatedly gave its quavering alarm call in the distance. Traditionally this call is supposed to guide the tiger to its kill, of which the jackal partakes later on, and in my heated imagination it seemed to tell the tigress that I was there and would sooner or later have to return through the thick cover below. But as the alarm call faded away, I realized that the tigress would not return. I therefore descended and made my way home.

Six months later, a deputation of Sikhs arrived at Tiger Haven, and announced that the uncle of one of the local farmers had been killed by the tigress while he was stripping cane. It was her eighth victim. I gathered that the body had been recovered, and that the tigress had taken shelter in a field of sugarcane. Since the field she had entered was now being watched from every side, she could not move out without being seen.

The Sikhs had travelled twenty miles by tractor to bring me the news, and it was late afternoon by the time we got back to the cane field. We discovered that the tigress was still inside. The field in which she had taken shelter was an isolated one of about one acre. The obvious retreat was to the south towards a low-lying marsh strip lined with tall sacchrum grass running east and west. Between the grass and the sugarcane the owner had cut a swathe three to five yards wide to serve as a fire line. I took up a position at the end of this corridor, so that I could have a good view if the tigress broke diagonally from the western end.

A line of Sikhs then beat the field starting from the far side, and shortly after they had reached half way, the tigress came out into the open at a slow canter, at the southern corner. Fortunately, I had a ·500 Express black powder rifle with a flat foresight, and using this eleven-pound weapon like a shotgun I fired a snap-shot before she disappeared into the long grass. It was impossible to tell whether she had been hit, and an inspection of the place where she had crossed the fire line revealed no blood. But two men sitting on a tree had seen the tigress jump at the shot. Our next move was to try and drive her out of the grass. This would be more difficult, and could be dangerous if she were wounded. At the other end of the marsh was a dhak (*Butea monosperma*) tree with a branch overlooking a water channel, and it was here that I took up my new position. But though I heard a twig crack below me in the channel, which led into a ravine, where incidently I had heard the alarm call of the jackal while I was sitting over the corpse of Bhaillu, nothing appeared. Dusk was now falling, and I decided that there was nothing more that I could do that day.

Next morning I returned to the channel and entered the ravine, and discovered a secluded grassy spot shaded by bushes and stunted trees. Obviously the tigress had used this as a den for some time, and it was from this direction that I had heard the jackal cry six months before. There were blood smears in two places where she had shifted her position, perhaps during the beat the previous evening. Sometime during the night she had left this cover. Her pugmarks were clearly imprinted in the ashes of the grass which had been burnt, and led towards the marsh further to the west. Mounting Bhagwan Piari, I advanced carefully through the deep water and clumps of narkul grass (*Arundo donax*) into the marsh. There I found the tigress sitting in the water with her hindquarters so badly inflamed that she was barely able to move. She just managed to stand up as the elephant approached her.

She measured eight feet nine inches between pegs, and was an old animal judging by her worn canines and incisors, but she had no visible disability. Driven out of her habitat, a shortage of wild prey species had forced her to survive on domestic stock, and ultimately familiarity had made her accept the human as a prey species. Perhaps rearing a family had forced her into human contact.

8 Long Toes,
or the Maneater of the
Nagrol-Neora River Basin

KAWAGHATTIA is a wooden pile bridge over the river Neora. The forest road descends from the escarpment which runs latitudinally along the length of the Park, and overlooks a bend in the river. Dense outcrops of narkul and elephant grass form an extensive marsh known as the Hulaskhani Bhagar, much used by tigers as a permanent residence during the hot season, and as a temporary refuge during the winter. Traditionally, a family of tigers was always located here.

The declaration of the National Park had always been unpopular with the Forest Department, with whom timber values were a top priority, and they resented that a forested area whose main qualification was the quality of their *Shorea Robusta* timber had been included as a wildlife refuge. They had fought a rearguard action against the insistence of a wildlife-oriented Prime Minister, and had given way with extreme reluctance to the stoppage of exploitation of the valuable Sal. Their final effort was a proposal that the extraction of wind-fallen Sal from the Park be permitted but, as this was a flagrant violation of the sanctity of a National Monument, I opposed such a proposal strongly. I have related in an earlier chapter the subterfuge by which the Chairman of the National Park Committee circumvented my opposition.

The timber-extraction operation was to be carried out by the Forest Corporation—a branch of the Department. The wind-blown timber was to be pulled out of the forest by bullock and buffalo carts to a central depot, and then loaded on to trucks and transported to base, and the operation was hopefully to be completed in two months. A camp was established overlooking the Hulaskhani Bhagar, and two hundred carts with their attendant animals and humans settled in. Soon the sylvan surroundings were permeated with the foetid malodour of residence, the singular hallmark of human occupation.

Tigers have very strong attachments to their residential habitat. The habitat is a selective occupance and the tiger has a strong disinclination to move out, subject to tigerine quality requirements; they will remain in residence as long as possible. Such a residential habitat was the Hulaskhani Bhagar and the surrounding area; and the stench of resident humanity, and the disturbance of habitat was excessively offensive, but had the attraction of the presence of domestic stock as prey. Soon tigers took to prowling around the encampment, and during the evening of 2 March 1978 a cartman named Akbar went to relieve himself near an outcrop of narkul grass on the banks of the river upstream of Kawaghattia. He folded his lungi, and placed it near himself, where I found it the next day. The tiger killed him and dragged him for about twenty yards, but did not attempt to feed. He abandoned the kill on the approach of a search party, and killed a bullock tethered to a cart near by. The following morning I found Akbar's blood-stained lungi lying to one side. Close by were the pugs of Long Toes, a sibling of Tara's Male who shared the Tiger Haven Range with him and Tara.

The next kill was in the catchment area of the Nagrol and Neora rivers. The Nepal border, which always had continuous forests with India, had been deforested by the Nepalese, and had been settled with ex-soldiers with firearms in their possession, which they used for poaching inside Indian territory. They also used to intrude into India to graze their cattle, and collect firewood. On 3 April one Dharamdatta Pandit went on some nefarious intrusion to the banks of the river Nagrol, where he was seized by a tiger. The next day his relatives found his rib-cage, which they removed for cremation. On my visit that evening I found the pugmarks of Long Toes, who had obviously moved further west from his first killing of Akbar at Kawaghattia. However, with his pugmarks were those of a tigress and two cubs, whose pugmarks were so small as to suggest that they had not been weaned. But it was fairly obvious that she had also fed, and that the tiger was killing for his family. Surprisingly enough, a second Nepali called Padam Bahadur went three days later to within a mile or so of the same spot on the Nagrol and he was also killed. The Director of the Park got word of the accident and went to the scene with some wildlife guards, and from the safety of a tree he watched the tiger pull the corpse into some tall grass, from where he could hear the crunch of bones, which the animal continued to chew even after they shouted and threw branches at him. The Director, however, was heard to remark that he wanted to shoot the tiger, although permission to destroy him would have to come from the Chief Wildlife Warden. Later on, I put the other facet of the problem to him, namely, that the these men who were killed used to poach and steal forest produce, and belonged to a foreign country, and the tiger was doing the job without the pay of forest guards. He did not concur. My visit later confirmed that the tigress had also shared the kill.

The final kill was of a Tharu tribal named Birja, in the same vicinity. He was supposed to be simple-minded, and was said to have strayed from his companions to have a drink in the river, from where he had been putting out a fire. No attempt had been made to recover the body as I presume he had no relatives. I followed the drag for some distance along the dry bed of the river to where the tiger had fed, but thereafter I found that the tigress had taken over. Further along, among a pile of débris left by flood waters, I found the tonsured head of the tribal, his hair licked clean by the rasping tongue of the tiger, his staring and terror-stricken eyes embedded in the stark skull, a forlorn reminder of a tragic midnight drama and the battle for survival.

I had come to know these river catchment areas well when searching for Prince, my male leopard who had opted for freedom in 1973. The Nagrol and Neora rivers meandered through dense undergrowth and tall Sal trees. The valuable timber had never been artificially transplanted, and here in this prime forest where the leopard had sought his freedom the regeneration was good, and the canopy a close one. In this twilight forest Prince had once roamed in the company of a black leopard, a rarity in these parts, and now in my search for maneater kills I would often come across Long Toes, immersed up to his eyebrows in water. My thought processes were weighted by questioning; I was aware that he was a maneater or, rather, had eaten men. I knew he could see me and was not wary, as he sat in the water and did not spring out when he saw me, as most tigers would have done. Though he had eaten humans, he also lived on other prey. What were *his* thought processes? Was he considering me as a prospective meal? Though he appeared unafraid, he never made a hostile move, and on one occasion when I was going on to a machan which I had put up to observe his activities, he was coming the opposite way and must have seen me for he never appeared.

Though Project Tiger had been in operation since 1973, and they did not agree that tigers could be weaned away from maneating, the

Director accepted my suggestion that the tigers should be provided with bait to tide over the lean periods when they were nurturing cubs. Burnt ambush cover and excessive human intrusion compounded the difficulties of capturing sufficient prey for the suckling tigress. Baits were therefore put out regularly near a wooden bridge on the Nagrol river. Maneating cases thereupon ceased dramatically, and at the end of the monsoon season the tiger family with two well grown cubs did not appear to need human sustenance. This is one of the few cases in which the human has allowed a tiger's natural disinclination to eat man act as a disincentive to so-called aberrant behaviour. The human in his arrogance even assumes that his flesh is delectable to tigers.

9 *The Median Tigress*

DURING the period when Tara's Male was courting Tara, a strange tigress appeared on the Range. She dragged a chital, which had been killed by a Fishing Cat in some sugarcane, across the river and into some dense cover, where she consumed the entire kill. The kill was a medium-sized doe, and killing it was a big effort for the cat, and her disappointment at this larceny was evident. Next day, the sounds of tigers mating echoed across the river, and I was left wondering how Tara was mating in the wild when she was just over two years old. That night Long Toes passed along the dirt track to the south of the Soheli. The way he swivelled his rump to spray bushes on either side of the road indicated that he was aware of what was going on in the bushes the other side of the stream, but there was no attempt at aggression, even though scribes are at pains to point out that tigers fight to the death over tigresses in season. Though Long Toes had been a victor over his sibling in a brief scuffle at a kill, he made no effort to dispossess his brother, and although he briefly crossed the river to the other side, he soon reappeared to continue his advance down the road, swivelling his hindquarters from side to side while spraying, to show his awareness at what was going on.

The next day my brother was coming to Tiger Haven when a lean tigress crossed the road. Tara's erstwhile Assistant Keeper was in the car and got down to call her, whereupon she turned round to sit down and look at him. However, by the time he came to call me Tara had disappeared, but on my call Long Toes appeared, and it became evident that Tara's Male was mating another tigress, and Tara had attached herself to Long Toes.

After the mating, Tara's Male returned to Tara in a mutual attraction, which is not the prerogative of humans only. About six months later, I came across signs of a chital kill by a tiger. Following the blood trail and damaged bushes, we came upon signs of a single cub, and soon found splinters of bone, which is all that remained of the chital. But there was no sign of the tigress, whom I now named the Median Tigress in absentia. A few days later my tracker went to investigate with a companion, and was followed by the tigress who demonstrated at them as they came out on to the road. It appeared that she had started developing aggressive tendencies, for some time later she killed a forest labourer who had strayed off the road to pick up some firewood; but as is usual with first human kills, she did not eat any portion though the single cub was reported to be with her, and was now about eighteen months old.

Her next kill was an assistant tracker of mine, by name Lallu. I was away at the time and Lallu followed the pugmarks of a tigress who had crossed the river and walked away east in the morning. She became aware of his approach and took cover behind a tree on the river bank. She crept up and sprang on him, and dragged him into cover, but only ate his genitals. As may be imagined, I was devastated on my return to think that Tara might have been responsible, but in my absence no action had been taken. However, the Median and her daughter continued to prey on chital, though another human was killed in the vicinity of the railway station at Dudhwa.

In November 1980 the tigress killed a sweepress outside the Dudhwa Forest Lodge in the early morning. By the time an elephant arrived to dispossess her of her kill she had dragged the body into some bushes and eaten the breasts. Her appetite whetted by what she had eaten, she crept into a ravine which was situated beneath the elephant stable of the Park. Here she must have lain all afternoon listening to the bustle above. In the afternoon at about 4 p.m., Asghar, an elephant *charkatta* or fodder cutter, went as luck would have it into the ravine to answer a call of nature. The tigress seized him and dragged him away. It was reported to me immediately, but darkness was falling and we were unable to find the carcass. Next morning the body was recovered. It had been half eaten, and the Park Director soon arrived, having been summoned from his headquarters at Lakhimpur.

Asghar's body had been removed and a young buffalo tied up as bait. I sat up on a machan with the Director, but the tigress did not return during the night. In the morning I circled the premises where the body had lain, but the elephant made no sign to indicate that the tigress was in the vicinity. After I returned to Tiger Haven the tigress appeared out of the grass and started calling, apparently in protest at the removal of her kill. She crossed the Palia-Dudhwa Road, skirted the forest barrier and walked down the metalled road to the Nepal border, calling loudly while doing so. Two miles down the road she turned right along a jungle track where she was joined by her daughter. The Director had followed her mounted on an elephant, but was unable to take any action because of his inexperience, and also because he was armed with a smooth bore shotgun borrowed from a Wildlife Guard, and loaded with buckshot which, incidentally, did not go off when test-fired later on. I was immediately summoned, but the tigress and cub had disappeared by the time I arrived.

In the evening I tethered a bait at the spot where she had branched off, and it was killed and partially eaten during the night. Next morning, the Director and I mounted an elephant and prepared to follow the drag as the tigress had broken the tethering rope. A ·375 Magnum owned by the Forest Department had meantime arrived for the Director from headquarters. An ill-maintained weapon with a broken safety catch, it was not a very impressive firearm, but the Director maintained that in his official position he should be allowed to shoot the tigress. On my query as to whether he felt confident, he said that he had been a good marksman at target practise.

We followed the drag and a tiger got up. The Director pointed his rifle but I restrained him as it was the cub. After a while the tigress appeared and sat down in front of the elephant. From her very boldness it was obvious that she was the main actress in the drama which had now entered its second phase. Encouraged by my permission, the Director fired a shot at the sitting tigress and she bounded off. My immediate reaction was one of regret that I had allowed this inexperienced and inept marksman to bungle a shot at point-blank range. However, we quartered the direction in which the tigress had taken off and, after some time, came upon her recumbent body. I could see a wound on her lower stomach and remember wondering how that amateurish shot had anchored the animal. I got the Director to fire another shot, and dismounted to pull the tigress' tail to check if she was dead. On joining me on the ground the Director asked me if it was Tara, which I denied. The matter was then closed, and I returned home. The cause of death continued to exercise my mind, and I returned next morning to the killing site. There I found that an inch-thick branch had been drilled by the rifle bullet; the mystery was explained. The bullet had been deflected and the gunshot changed direction to pierce the tigress' heart. The Director's luck had held. I walked down to the Park Headquarters and presented the severed branch to him, instead of keeping it myself, with the remark that he had been lucky with his shot! For without the aid of the twig he might have missed altogether.

The Director had assured me that he would bury the tigress where she lay, to protect the worsening image of the tiger; but on arrival I discovered that he had other plans. A jeep trailer had been loaded with freshly cut green grass, and packed into the greenery lay the beautiful tigress as if deeply asleep, her ugly wounds covered. He had decided to take her on a triumphal flagmarch to headquarters through the principal towns of the district. I then knew that the emotion and confusion existed only in my mind. This was a monster who had sinned, not against natural laws but against those of her destroyers. Even as I watched, the trailer swung out behind the jeep on its image-building safari. It stopped at every town and played hard to the gallery. People gazed at the slaughtered monster and the hero who had rid the people of a great fear.

Yet the hot air shot off along the way was nothing to that generated at headquarters in Lucknow. The skin was fully mounted at government expense and gratefully presented to the Director. Posing in front of the stuffed body, he invited journalists to write up the story. Wildly fanciful accounts related how he had been charged by the tigress in his residence. He wrote articles encouraging readers to conclude that the killed tigress was Tara, and told how I had dismounted after she had been shot, with tears supposedly brimming in my eyes. My denial did not feature at all, nor did the fact that I had lived with Tara for a year and a half counterbalance the accusations of people, some of whom had never seen Tara as a living entity. The story is still current among Departmental officials who, while questioning the right of animals to exist while humans starve, lack the empathy (which lies within me) to appreciate the suffering of an animal.

10 The Maneater of Barauchha Nala

THE complex stages of evolution down the ages are in the main an account of predator/prey relations influenced by environmental conditions. The prey base is the ultimate determinant of the morphology of the predator. The dinosaurs of prehistory had gigantic ungulates like the brontosaurus and dimorphodons, who were preyed upon by the tyrannosaurus and the allosaurus, whose relicts now remain in the form of the crocodilian of the present world. Assisted by the pressure of the ice ages a branch of the current mammalian forms evolved from their reptilian ancestors into the larger sabre tooths and *Panthera Atrox*, and their prey species of large deer and ox-species. Over the millennia they have once more evolved into the present master predators in the shape of the lion and tiger. With the evolution of the master predators, the lesser hunters in the form of the jaguar, leopard, mountain lion and cheetah, as well as numerous lesser cats, have established their own niches of existence.

The process of evolution still goes on, but whereas in the past the extinction of a species took place once in a generation, we are working towards a record of perhaps one a year under the influence of an uncontrolled human population surge, and increasing demands to sustain that burgeoning population. The effect of environmental influences is an infinite one as far as the predators are concerned, and it is fascinating to theorize whether the two master predators could conceivably exchange roles, whereby the lion, supposedly the only social cat, could become solitary because of the exigencies of prey utilization, as has happened in the case of the Barbary Lion, whereas the tiger could become visible interacting in a pride. The African lion has to be social because he lives in a plains' habitat. Prey species are numerous, and in many cases too large to be subdued by a single lion. The terrain is an open one, and the kill has got to be demolished immediately, otherwise scavengers will have a weightage which will preclude them from becoming part-time predators and playing a role in controlling the locally migratory populations among the antelopes which is a feature of the African plains. Plains' animals, presumably under the influences of synchronous breeding dynamics, increase much faster than animals who dwell in closed habitats, and the spotted hyena, looked down upon as a lowly scavenger, is actually a predator in his own right, controlling prey populations according to the universal distillate wisdom of the survival of the fittest. The lesser cats of Africa could never conceivably become specialized predators, and their predatory function must always remain under the dominant influence of the senior cat.

Tigers live in a closed habitat, where prey species are by and large comparatively small, and not prolific, and their consumption is not influenced by the presence of scavengers. Moreover, plentiful cover enables them to hide prey from the prying eyes of scavengers; thus, they finish what they kill, and suckling tigresses can wean their offspring to a diet of raw flesh. Though a suspicion exists that cats regurgitate for their offspring, as far as I am aware no visual proof exists to prove the contention. In areas of plentiful prey, tigers are tolerant in familial groups, which are really the nucleus of the lion pride, and tigresses with a common blood line often associate with each other. Even the leopards in Sri Lanka, where they are the leading predator in the absence of the tiger, have a tendency towards socializing, though the Tamil Tiger terrorists have played havoc with any social structure which might have been evolving.

The great cats have enormous powers of adaptability, and have accepted environmental changes with remarkable aplomb. Impelled by the pressures of the ice ages and expanding populations, tigers have colonized most of Asia. From the record weight of 845 pounds of *P.T. Altaica* in Siberia shot in the Sikhote Alin mountains in 1950, tigers have metamorphosed to a possible 200 pounds in the form of *P.T. Balica.* Yet four out of their eight subspecies have gone. From a predominance of pure white underparts on a pale buff, broken striped background, in keeping with the Russian Taiga, the southern races are generally dark with complete black stripes on a tawny orange background. Though garishly distinctive when viewed in isolation, they have merged with their habitat over the generations, which assists them in ambush operations in heavy cover. They are low slung and closer to the true cat than the lion, who compares with them in size and weight. He stands taller than the tiger to enable him to oversee the short grasses of his habitat, but has a lesser girth of limb. As he moves behind the pride looking for all the world like a moving haystack, his size and ponderous dignity relegate the lion to the predominant role of maintaining the integrity of the pride and the female is the huntress. They rest for twenty hours out of twenty-four and, as a writer puts it, look like honey poured upon the golden plains. They are Africa, and as George Adamson put it, as their roars rumble across the veldt at evenfall, they are saying: WHO IS LORD OF THIS LAND? WHO IS LORD OF THIS LAND? I AM! I AM! I AM! When they are gone, Africa will have lost its magic.

The leopard is the quintessential cat, unsurpassed pound for pound in athleticism, power and beauty. Its matched skin-coat has sold for 25,000 dollars, which production was estimated as being the life-time breeding effort of a pair of leopards. Its adaptability has allowed it to live in habitats from rain forest to arid rocks and plains; its catholicity of dietary demands has enabled it to survive on birds, and rodents, and seemingly to live forever. Yet lacking the symbolism of his seniors, the leopard must now pay for his own survival in an operation of attrition which can delay, but not deter. Sub-Saharan Africa has produced a computer estimate of 700,000–900,000 leopards to justify a sustained yield, and even Nepal, with most of its wildlife habitat gone, wishes to have a Leopard Quota under the guidance of the American hunters' lobby. International conservation bodies say that quotas on the commercial hunting of predators who are a menace to livestock will save the goose which lays the golden egg. But for how long? Their backs are to the wall.

An account of the activities of the maneating tigress of Barauchha Nala illustrates the last stand of a master predator, and how compulsions drove her to human confrontations, and ultimate and compulsory destruction for not obeying man-made laws. A complete reorientation of management principles must be devised for Project Tiger under international direction. The tiger is a key species for the preservation of the environment, but it can only exist if isolated from human endeavour.

The Gola forest (not to be confused with Ghola) is linked with the Kishanpur Sanctuary (now part of the Dudhwa Tiger Reserve) by a narrow corridor of forest and grassland along the Ul river. The remaining privately-owned grasslands and mixed forest have been mainly reclaimed for sugarcane plantation, and prey species largely eradicated for purposes of crop protection. A few habitat areas remain along the river, but these are flooded during the monsoon, further reducing the perennial cover and converting sugarcane into an ersatz but strictly seasonal refuge. Thanks to heavy human use through grazing domestic stock and the collection of grassland thatching material, fire is extensively employed and virtually no understorey of shrubbery exists in the remaining Sal and mixed forests. Furthermore, the slow maturity processes of Sal and its gradual replacement by steel for railway fishplates and girders, is leading to its substitution by quick-maturing varieties like eucalyptus and teak. About 15 kilometres to the west, and separated by cultivation is an isolated patch of forest along the Kathina river, with suitable habitat areas, but no wild prey species. Despite the replacement of grassland cover by sugarcane and the decimation of wild prey, resident tigers stayed on, but increasingly came into conflict with human interests. Isolated instances of human killings occurred in chance encounters, and a male and a female were shot in an irresponsible effort to eliminate the alleged maneater as soon as possible. Unfortunately, an expert committee appointed to investigate the maneating problem had also recommended that it did not matter if the wrong tigers were eliminated in the haste to get rid of the actual maneater, and that even the use of poison was a permissible remedy to the problem.

The tigress claimed her first human victim in 1978 on 15 March. Bhagwan Din went alone to cut fodder along the banks of the Ul river. A few scattered bones were discovered the next day, close to the decaying carcass of a wild boar killed by the tigress earlier. Later, traces of a 2–3 month old cub were found, and it was obvious that paucity of prey and familiarization had impelled the suckling mother to accept the human as prey. The next morning a beat was organized to flush out the tigress, but she mauled one of the beaters in defence of her cub who was presumably cached close by. Though a certain minimal wild prey population did exist in the Gola forests, the tigress had now accepted the human as a prey species, and when on 3 April Nokhey Lal went to cut grass along the Barauchha Nala, a tributary of the Ul, he was eaten. Next day the tigress killed Chetram a kilometre away from her kill of the previous day and within sight of two other grass cutters, who shouted and were able to recover the carcass with the assistance of others. Human killings are always liable to snowball, as rescue operations occur only where possible, leading to extra victims.

Thereafter, alarmed by continual pursuit and disturbance, the tigress shifted, carrying her cub to the Kathina forest, which meant a journey of about 15 kilometres across open fields, but into an area with no wild prey, and where a conflict with human interests was inevitable. Here she killed Jhau while he was harvesting wheat on 12 April and dragged him into some cane-brake thickets for about 150 metres, and ate half of him. Two days later she killed Chote Das, who had gone in search of his cattle, and ate all of him except for a leg and his head.

I was now invited by the Director of the Dudhwa National Park to visit the area where the killings had erupted. On arrival at the Barauchha Nala site I was greeted by extensive human activity. The Plantation Division of the Forest Department was engaged in what was known as 'clear felling' of Sal forests that were to be replaced by quick-growing varieties by impatient overnight planners. Stately 'seeding' timbers of 150 to 200 years of age were toppled, to be substituted by spindly eucalyptus, which lowered the water table and whose cultural operation kept the understorey free of cover. A commercial forester's delight! In addition, a two-year lease was granted to large-scale farmers, who planted agricultural crops in planted areas. Unsavoury characters like 'Shikari Babu' who, under pretence of guarding Departmental plantations, slaughtered wildlife with unlicenced firearms and sold the meat in the local market, and his elder brother, who was arrested for selling arms to a prominent dacoit and got himself exonerated by presenting a subvention to the local Revenue Minister, were prominent among these two-year lease holders.

The tigers were disturbed by these shock operations, and as habitat retreats and wild prey diminished, they came increasingly into conflict with human interests. A dismaying development took place in the proposed capture of so-called aberrant animals and their incarceration in zoos. Shooting tigers had been made illegal in 1972, and the declaration of maneaters earmarked for destruction was a complicated one. Moreover, accomplished hunters were on the decline, and volunteers were increasingly difficult to come by. The tiger had been nominated as the national animal. I had also proposed that tigers which had been disoriented by degraded habitat should be translocated to other suitable areas. However, by devious reasoning, the Project officials had accepted the immobilizing capture of aberrant tigers but recommended that they should be sent to zoos, on the invidious plea that a translocated animal may not be acceptable to local residents in their capacity as territorial animals. The argument that in any case by capture they were destroying the tiger in his original habitat and that it was infinitely preferable for conspecifics to decide on acceptance or rejection than for the human to be judge, jury and irresponsible executioner, was not accepted. However, in reality the capture and imprisonment of an animal with the symbolism of the tiger became a source of earning cheap acclaim on the cocktail circuit; it pandered to the tastes of the local inhabitants, and misled international forums into believing that a tiger had been saved, when in reality it had been destroyed in its habitat. Four tigers thus captured died in the Lucknow Zoo, but Operation Imprison Tiger still continued.

The Research Officer of the Corbett National Park was detailed to tranquillize the Barauchha tigress, but he proved singularly inept at the operation and was only successful on a trial darting of a chital doe, who subsequently died, because he had forgotten to bring an antidote with him! On my arrival at Barauchha I was informed that plans were afoot to shoot the tigress, but on my further investigation I was informed by Shikari Babu that there were five other tigresses and one tiger. My query as to how they were going to identify the maneating tigress did not appeal to them, and I was not invited to participate in further activities. However, in the ensuing witch-hunt, a male and female were destroyed, but killings still continued.

At one time it was conjectured that there were two maneaters operating—one in the Gola area of the Barauchha Nala, and the other 15 kilometres away, along the Kathina river. The main reason for this surmise was that the two operational areas were separated by cultivation. However, as there was a synchrony between the killings it became apparent that, thanks to the disturbed and degraded habitat, the tigress had opted for the superior habitat conditions along the Kathina river, despite the fact that there was no wild game—she was suckling cubs, and therefore needed undisturbed cover. Such a pattern of existence was confirmed by the fact that, after her kill of Chote Das, on 14 April 1979 in the Kathina catchment, she killed and partially devoured Sibram on the banks of the Ul, where he had gone to fish on 9 June, or nearly two months after the previous kill.

Her next human kill, also in the Gola reserved forest, was on 14 October, or over four months later, and a search next morning revealed the scattered remains of Kailash, a farm labourer, but close to which was lying a fresh kill of a wild boar. The tigress was alternating between the Gola and Kathina forests in an endeavour to rationalize an existence which was increasingly disrupted by constant pursuit. She killed Duber, a labourer who was cutting fodder on the edge of the Gola forests on 22 October, but in the ensuing hue and cry, when tractors joined in the search, she was forced to abandon her kill, and then killed and ate Ram Adhin on the banks of the Kathina on 25 October, 15 kilometres away; but she returned two months later on 27 December to kill and devour Tauley. It was also confirmed by the intervals between human killings that the tigress was living on other forms of prey, for which she had to rely mainly on the Gola forests.

During the early months of 1979 her life was further complicated by the fact that she mothered another family, a year after she had given birth to a single cub, for which she was obliged to seek the comparatively undisturbed cover of the Kathina catchment, and also kill more than she needed when getting an opportunity to do so. A small cub was seen during the search for Lakshman who had gone into the forest to collect fruit on 1 February. Later, she killed and ate Chetram at midday on 13 February.

Breeding dynamics have established that normally free-ranging tigresses have families every two years or so, depending on oestrus conditions and the availability of a dominant male. Therefore, a year's interval between parturition meant that, thanks to the restricted habitat in the Gola forest, the female was constantly exposed to the androus pheromones of the male which induced an early receptivity. As will be appreciated, the appearance of a second generation of cubs intensified the difficult life of the nursing mother, and increased her feeding demands. Fortunately, the previous singleton cub was male and could be expected to branch out on his own at 16–18 months.

Efforts at immobilization were unsuccessful, and a baited drop cage was also not successful in capturing the tigress as she clawed portions of the unfortunate bait from the outside. Therefore, buffaloes were tied out with the intention of shooting the tigress. On 28 May, Ram Das slept out in the open next to a crop of sugarcane and a diesel pump for irrigating his field. Why he committed such a foolhardy act is not understandable as everyone was aware that the maneating tigress was in the vicinity, and that bait was being put out regularly. Three bullocks were tethered in proximity. In the early hours of the morning the tigress appeared with the elder cub, and a younger one, and killed two bullocks, mauling the third. Presumably hearing the shouts of alarm from Ram Das, she overpowered him and dragged him over a kilometre into dense cover, from where his body was recovered with the genitals and one leg devoured. The maneater was now so bold that she had frontally attacked Ram Das on her thirteenth human kill. Famished and pressurized in her efforts to feed two generations of cubs in increasingly adverse habitat conditions and diminishing natural prey species, she had really gone on a rampage in the pre-dawn hours of 28 May. She was shot the next evening after killing a live bait which was tethered at the place where Ram Das' body had been recovered. She was a young and undernourished tigress. That night the elder cub, who was probably about sixteen months old, was heard calling, and later came to drag the kill into some dense cover along the Kathina. In the evening, the Director of the Park waited with a tranquillizer gun, but the cub did not put in an appearance.

In early June unsuccessful efforts were made to locate the cubs, though the elder one had been seen chasing a Nilgai in an inexperienced effort to make a kill. If baiting for the elder cub had been continued, there is no doubt that the cubs would have been located, but such concern was not felt by the forest authorities and the two cubs were found lying in a pit on 26 June, 200 metres from where the elder cub had dragged and eaten the mother's kill; no doubt they had snacked before it was eaten out. The female cub was dead, and the male cub survived for three days before he, too, succumbed on the exhausting journey to Lucknow.

On the night of 1–2 July the elder male cub got isolated in a mango grove about 20 kilometres from the Kathina forest. He was seen by the villagers; and one Pandit Amarnath, the possessor of a gun, was killed while trying to shoot the tiger. The police were informed and they cordoned off the grove and set fire to it. The tiger rushed out and killed another villager. Later, the station officer in charge of the Mikelganj Police Station arrived with a posse of policemen. They drafted all available firearms, and fired a total of 150 rounds into the grove, without result. One hopes that the cub made his way to Kishanpur, and still lives as an elderly tiger of the Sixteenth Tiger Reserve.

The foregoing blow-by-blow account of the rise and fall of the Barauchha Nala Maneater is a poignant example of how tigers are being crowded against the wall. The erosion of habitat and prey species, their enforced acceptance of a foreign prey species, and the unwillingness, rather inability, to accept man-made laws illustrate that tigers must exist in isolation, and cannot do so as competitors to humans. Any attempt at an integration with human interests is bound to have repercussions. The incidence of wildlife conservation must be looked after by a dedicated band of administrators, and not as the concomitant of a commercial operation. To say that wildlife must be looked after by foresters because animals live in forests is to say that the Finance Department should be looked after by the Ministry of Works and Housing. There must be a separate Wildlife Service to look after wildlife, and the tiger must be considered as the symbolic biotic apex which will ensure the sanctity of the ecosystem over which he holds sway.

11 The Ghola Maneater

GHOLA was once maintained as a hunting reserve by Lionel Hearsey, from whose brother, George, I had leased 750 acres when establishing my original farm at Jasbirnagar. It is a landholding of 3,000 acres, bounded to the south by the Naudha Bhagar, and to the west and north by the Soheli stream which is the boundary of the present Dudhwa National Park. The Naudha Bhagar, which is in reality a marshy river, and its various ramifications, was the favoured habitat of swampdeer, and a successive bastion in their retreat from the catchment of the Sarda river as cultivation took over from the wilderness. Flood waters had their drainage by the various distributaries into the Park river of the Neora, but the Ghola lake retained its modicum of water and was increasingly frequented by the barasingha. In Chapter 2 I have related how I attempted to persuade the authorities to convert Ghola into a refuge for the swampdeer. Unfortunately the unwillingness of the State government to take time by the forelock enabled lawless elements to colonize this land and created the problems of maneating. The dwindling numbers of barasingha, who migrate out of the Park with the monsoon, now get shot.

One night in early winter, Shiv Shankar lay in a straw lean-to in Ghola, protecting his master's sugarcane field from grazing ungulates and himself from the chill of a foggy night. He was covered with a quilt and an oil lamp hung suspended from the roof. Suddenly a tiger appeared out of the Stygian darkness, and seized him through the quilt. Fortunately, the tiger got hold of him by the thigh, and in the convulsive struggle the lamp overturned, setting ablaze the paddy straw on which Shiv Shankar rested. The tiger decamped. Some days later, by an amazing coincidence, Shiv Shankar was seized by the same tiger while stripping cane. He was saved by the fact that his companion cane strippers all shouted, and also because he had a long piece of cloth wound round his head so that he merely suffered a severe scalp wound and was not fatally injured—thereby possibly creating a record for the *Guinness Book* as the only man to escape twice from the jaws of the world's most powerful predator.

A few days later the tiger struck again, seizing a girl outside her hut about a mile away. She was dead by the time her body was recovered. Later, a cultivator went to level his field before sowing. He had two buffaloes yoked to a plank upon which he stood to guide the animals and make the levelling more effective. The buffaloes were working up and down a field at right angles to a field of short, green grass, alongside which was a plantation of sugarcane. A tiger emerged from the sugarcane and crouched in the short grass. As the buffaloes turned away, the tiger launched an attack on his selected victim, and seized the man and started to drag him into the cover without pausing to kill him. Rescuers ran shouting to his aid as he was borne yelling and clamped in the jaws of his destroyer. Though the tiger dropped him, he was dead by the time assistance arrived.

These incidents were reported to the Forest Department who, by some peculiar process of deduction, declared the maneater to be a tigress, possibly because it had been postulated that it is more likely that tigresses become maneaters during their stressful existence while nursing cubs. Baited cages were now put out in various sugarcane fields in the hope of trapping the maneater and sending it to a zoo. For such capture had become a status achievement with the imprisonment of the Bangajhala tiger caught outside the Corbett National Park, in its buffer zone. However, when I went to inspect the sugarcane area where the trap had been set, I found the pugmarks of no less than a family of four tigers, two of whom were males. I was therefore filled with a foreboding, but my query as to how the Department were going to ensure the capture of the maneater when they did not know the identity of the culprit was unanswerable. Inevitably, one night a tiger entered the cage and was caught. No one dared to approach the cage at night and, typically, in the morning it was discovered that the only man capable of administrating a tranquillizing drug was away at headquarters, so that he was not able to get to the site of capture till 3 p.m. the next day. By then the animal had been in the cage for sixteen hours and, as news had spread, an estimated crowd of 10,000 people had poured out of Pallia and from the surrounding villages and farms to stare at it.

When the Research Officer of the Corbett National Park arrived eventually, he was unable to sedate the animal with his dart gun and the tranquillizing had to be done with a hypodermic syringe. Needless to say, the tiger was badly injured in its struggle to escape both before and after the Research Officer came on the scene. After it was rendered unconscious at last, the Research Officer took the animal's temperature by lifting its tail and inserting a thermometer into its anus. Having completed this operation, while the crowd jostled for a view, he announced that the animal was a male, and that the female would have to be captured as well as she was the maneater. The tiger was taken to the Lucknow Zoo and there declared to be a tigress. The sexual organs of the big cats are so prominent that it seemed scarcely possible for the concerned officer to have made such a mistake, yet incredibly the Zoo maintained that the tiger was indeed a tigress. I need hardly add that human killings continued as before. The Forest Department, having failed to identify the animal, had condemned an innocent animal to penal servitude and a slow death. In order to maintain the charade, they placed the 'tigress' behind a screen, away from public gaze, on the spurious excuse that 'she' was upset by being stared at. The next development was the announcement that 'she' had died of snake-bite—in a concrete cage. A disgraceful and shameful episode in wildlife conservation was officially closed.

To say that I was taken aback by these developments was to put it mildly. Here was a clear instance of local authorities defying the law and ordering the imprisonment and death of an innocent animal in order to appease public anger and fear; and, of course, they advanced the specious excuse that by putting it behind bars they were saving it!

Soon after this incident, a man with his wife and child came to visit friends in Ghola. As the man squatted by the edge of a sugarcane field to urinate within sight of the hutment of the friends he had come to visit, a tiger seized and dragged him into the field. His friend set fire to the cane to scare the tiger off, but by the time they drove a tractor into the half-burnt field the man was dead. The sugarcane field belonged to a large farmer who, like other large farmers, lived in permanent residences at some distance from their landholdings, whereas their labourers resided in thatch structures close to the small fields some of them still had. Naturally, the local dwellers were upset and frightened by the death, and the situation was aggravated by the fact that the owner of the burnt sugarcane field resented his loss and, unable or unwilling to realize how terrifying existence had become in a place where a tiger had accepted humans as a legitimate form of prey, demanded compensation for the loss of cane he had suffered.

When I arrived on the scene the next morning, I was assailed by demands that the animal responsible for the crime be eliminated immediately. The people told me that it was a tigress, but on visiting the site of the death I found that the killer was a male. When the locals tried to assert their rights to the area by saying that they had lived in it for ten years, I did not endear myself to them by saying that the tigers had lived there for ten thousand. Stories about Tara had already made me unpopular, and now the old women of this apparently matriarchal society threatened to assault me on the grounds that I had started this wave of killing by introducing a hand-reared tigress into the National Park. A whole crowd of old crones surrounded me, screaming threats and abuse.

At a meeting of the Indian Board for Wildlife in 1981 I had suggested that a committee should be appointed to investigate the maneating problem which had erupted, and the committee arrived during the reign of the Ghola Maneater. An initial visit to the area produced the same raucous recriminations which I had been subjected to a few days earlier, and the committee felt constrained to report on my unpopularity with the local settlers despite the fact that I had assisted the latter by destroying 'maneaters' twenty years previously. They recommended the establishment of a Tiger Watch to observe the activities of potential 'aberrants' and to deal with proven 'maneaters'. They implied that the reason for the tiger-human confrontation was the success of conservation measures, plus the spread of uninhibited sugarcane plantations which had led to the destruction of wild prey species. However, they failed to appreciate that the destruction of prime tiger habitat in Nepal and the degradation of the legendary sub-montane holding grounds of the Churia Range had created an artificial tiger surplus which, once garnered, would be the cause of an irreversible plummeting of world tiger populations. Ten years later this is what happened here.

A local agitation engineered by political aspirants now started up. A farmer with political ambitions, who had earlier complained about Prince, my leopard, wrote in an open letter to the Prime Minister that, unless immediate action was taken by the Forest Department, he would, after a week's token fast, shoot the offending tigers himself. As a result, another tigress was declared a maneater, even though I had made it clear that the offending animal was a male; and the Director of the Dudhwa National Park was entrusted with its destruction.

He therefore put up a machan on a handy peepul tree (*Ficus religiosa*) and started sitting over a live bait. One night the bait was killed, but unfortunately the Director had gone away and the tiger ate most of the small buffalo. Next night the tiger arrived soon after 9 p.m. to finish his meal, but the remains had been carelessly tethered and he broke the rope and started to pull the carcass off into a nearby patch of sugarcane. The Director fired a hasty shot, which on inspection was found to have missed its target. Later that night, after the Director had left, the tiger returned and dragged the kill away and demolished it.

By now terror had gripped the entire community, as the people living in their fragile huts realized how vulnerable they were before a resolute tiger who now deliberately sought human prey. Fears were redoubled by the knowledge that the killer had not made a single meal off his last five human victims: he had thus killed more people than he needed to satisfy his hunger, and would certainly strike again as soon as opportunity presented. Soon he would be bold enough not to relinquish his quarry when challenged.

The Forest Department was blamed for not taking serious steps to destroy the tiger, but most of the anger was vented on me. People complained that I was protecting and encouraging the tigers, and that the man-eating had only begun since I released Tara. They also claimed that they were now haunted by the spirit of a farmer murdered years before in a land dispute, and that it could not be destroyed. Despite my point-blank assertion that the killer was a male, the officials of the Forest Department still maintained that it was a female. No doubt they hoped that, if they managed to shoot a tigress, they could claim that they had dispatched the hated Tara; the Department had never accepted that it was possible to return a hand-reared tiger cub to free living.

That evening another bait was tied out, and the Director again took his place on the machan. At 10 p.m. the tiger rushed out and seized the buffalo, but instead of waiting till the killing process was over and he had a steady target, the Director fired another hasty shot without any definite result. Next morning he came looking for me in a panic and asked me to take temporary charge of the hunt. Having driven home to collect my rifle and Jackson, my tracker, I proceeded to the scene of action. As we started investigations the atmosphere was tense, and scathing references to the ineptitude with which operations were being conducted ceased only when Jackson found a faint smear of blood. We then began the unpleasant task of trying to locate a wounded tiger inside the dense sugarcane.

As there was no visibility inside the cane field, it was not possible to follow up on foot, and a party of four elephants was assembled. We found that sometime during the night the tiger had emerged from the far end of the field but then turned back on his tracks into the shelter. There we found a few more blood smears. The unsheathed claws visible in the front left forepaw pugmarks showed that the wound was in the front foreleg, and was severe enough to prevent the animal from venturing into the open.

For some time we combed the field with elephants, until suddenly from underneath the feet of one of them the tiger gave a harsh snarl. The realization that he was very much alive shook many of the searchers mounted on the elephants, and instantly a vociferous argument broke out as to what should be done next. I said that, as we had now located the wounded animal, we must not lose contact but should close in and try to finish him off. The others, led by the Director, started edging away from where the tiger was located, and the badly trained elephants started fidgeting nervously.

I become exasperated and, since the operation was supposedly under the orders of the Forest Department, I could not give orders about what to do. So I decided to stand down from my position as temporary leader. Then someone advanced the suggestion that a tractor with a levelling plank should make lanes through the cane to improve visibility. This was an entirely irresponsible suggestion, as it would entail almost total destruction of the crop where the levelling took place. Moreover, this entailed a two-hour wait for a machine to be fetched, and the lethargy of inaction took over. By the time the tractor had come and a few lanes opened up, the owner of the field had also arrived and objected strongly to the havoc being caused to his crop, no matter however worthy the cause.

The rot had now set in, and once more everyone withdrew from the cane field. A temporary stalemate ensued, and everyone talked together. But soon tempers flared once more. The owner of the field slapped the tractor operator. The tractor owner took umbrage and fired a shot at the farmer from the security of the Director's elephant on which he was sitting, fortunately from a distance. He then sprang off the elephant and advanced on the field owner. For a while the maneater hunt took a back seat, and a fight between two factions of the Sikh community seemed imminent. I leapt off my elephant and physically restrained the advance of the tractor owner. No sooner had peace been restored than the local settlers attacked the Sikh farmer with sticks and stones for not allowing his cane field to be levelled. When he got into his jeep and drove off, they brought matters to a head by setting fire to his crop. As the vaulting flames leapt through the cane, the tiger was seen limping slowly and painfully across one of the lanes, and it seemed clear that he would not leave cover until he had to; and only when the field had burnt right out would he emerge. The elephants shifted uncomfortably as the tongues of flame flickered against the skyline. Sensing where the end would be, everyone who was armed dismounted, except for the Director and the tractor owner, who had once more mounted the elephant and formed a line across the northern end of the field where the blaze was obviously going to burn itself out, according to the prevailing breeze.

The death squad's formidable armament consisted of three ·375 Magnum rifles, one ·30–06, two ·315s and an assortment of smooth bores of ancient and unlicenced vintage. The marksmen formed the front line and, immediately behind, about two hundred local inhabitants waited eagerly for the grand finale. As the flames approached, the heat became intense even where we stood and we involuntarily edged away from the burning crop. In the end, only one triangular patch remained unburnt; and just as people were beginning to fear that the tiger had managed to double back in some mysterious way, two shots rang out from the Park Director and his accomplice, whose fidgeting elephant was some 200 yards off. Their only effect was to turn the tiger back into the cane. But at last he emerged in front of us with a defiant snarl.

At the first two shots he buckled and went down. Then he staggered to his feet again, but as I fired he crumpled and collapsed. A wild cheer rent the air, and everyone started firing in an unrestrained *feu de joie*. The release of an enormous tension was palpable. The Assistant Wildlife Warden, one Aftab Ali, carried away by the excitement ran forward still firing, till I yelled at him to desist. Rushing up to the fallen tiger he seized it by the tail and then, to show how little he feared it, launched a violent kick at its head. The next day I was amused to see that he was limping, and the day following he had his leg in plaster! The women who had previously threatened to assault me now hastened to garland me with tinsel, crying out '*Arjan Singh ki jai*'—'praise be to Arjan Singh'. Their sudden and violent change of mood reflected all too clearly the state of terror to which the maneater had reduced them.

The Maneater of Ghola was an average-sized male in his prime, and with no serious infirmity. A post mortem revealed that the first shot had broken his left shoulder, and under his skin were several charges of buckshot. Yet he had not been incapacitated. His sudden acceptance of an alien prey which had led to five human deaths, much destruction of property, and an incalculable amount of fear and stress, was caused by the fact that he had been thrust into the proximity of humans, and the violent reprisals to which he had been subjected to by them. Tigers live by violence, and though they are capable of restraint, their position of dominance in the natural scheme of existence encourages them to meet aggression with violence. Culpable though he was in human terms of having become a murderer, I could not suppress a pang of remorse at his passing, and the desperation in the defiant snarl as he emerged from the inferno to his doom haunted me for many days.

12 Suheli, the Maneating Tigress

DURING April 1985 a tourist mounted on a Park elephant was wandering in the vicinity of the Twin Lakes of the Dudhwa National Park in the never ending search for a sight of a tiger, which seems to be the focal point of every tourist's questing eye. It was therefore with a sense of achievement that the rider saw a tigress at the edge of some tall grass. The tigress was very thin, and was limping on her right foreleg. She sat down every few yards, but soon disappeared into the tall grass. I happened to meet this young man later in the morning, and he related his observations to me. I therefore went to inspect the site, as I was aware that Tara was bringing up her second family of two females, who were running their second year. I was also filled with apprehension that the suffering animal was likely to be one of her offspring. Examination of the precincts revealed the pugmarks of a small tigress, and it now remained to establish her identity. I tied up a buffalo bait to the west of Tiger Haven and it was killed by Tara that night.

Next afternoon, as I inspected the Neora river near the kill site, I saw a small head showing out of the water and, as the tigress limped along the stream, my fears were realized that the injured animal was indeed Tara's daughter by Tara's Male. It occurred to me that the obvious procedure was to immobilize her, examine her wound, and have her treated with a view to a subsequent release. I thus went to see the Director who was camping at a forest rest house in Sonaripur. He appeared very concerned, but said that if he was to recommend a course of action he would have to see the afflicted tigress. A young photographer was in residence with me making a film on Tara and, while he continued to film, the Director met me at Tiger Haven and I took him to the river site. The tigress behaved impeccably in displaying her disability, limped painfully along the stream, and disappeared into the forest in full view of the Director, this time walking on three legs. The Director promised to recommend a course of action to the Chief Wildlife Warden, whereby the tigress would be tranquillized and examined in order to decide a course of future action. I was encouraged to hope that meaningful action might be initiated, for though Mrs Gandhi had unfortunately passed from the scene I persuaded myself that her son Rajiv, who hopefully had inherited her enthusiasms, would agree to the procedure I suggested. However, as time wore on I realized that initiating action was going to be more difficult than getting promises. We had a Chief Wildlife Warden who believed that the proper place for a tiger was behind bars, and who indeed had the temerity to suggest that all free-ranging tigers outside the National Park should be trapped and sent to zoos. In fact, he had initiated a programme for trapping, and it was only on my insistence when I wrote to him 'It is not within your competence to order the capture of free-ranging tigers in order to send them to zoos' that he withdrew those blanket orders.

Days continued to pass while I awaited instructions and permission for the Director to commence operations in order to capture the animal; he had maintained that he was not empowered to undertake such action without the express authorization of his Chief. He thus took shelter behind the letter of the law, which he had no desire to circumvent for, as will be seen later, he could have done so had he so wished.

In the mean time weeks passed by without any positive action to assist the afflicted animal. Fortunately, I had been able to get the Director to agree to feeding the tigress until some action was taken, and I arranged for baits to be tied up which were killed by her mother, and upon which she also fed. Sometimes, of course, Tara was wandering elsewhere, while the young tigress was restricted in her wanderings not only because of her lameness, but because water gave her wounds relief and she would sit for hours in the shallow river. I watched her getting weaker, and her multiple wounds seemingly getting worse. She took to finding shelter in a shallow cave which had been formed by the licking of mineral salts by deer under the spreading roots of a ficus tree growing on the side of the escarpment. When she was not in the water or trying to assuage a hunger which must have been increasingly difficult to satisfy in the absence of Tara, she spent the time in this cave.

One day I was walking along the escarpment in my endeavour to keep in touch with Tara's daughter and, happening to pass the cave,

I peered in and was immediately greeted by an explosive snarl from the afflicted cub who was sheltering from the flies attracted to the open wounds which she licked avidly. I stepped back hurriedly, and watched the young tigress, now about seventeen months old, limp past me. Fortuitously, I heard the swish of branches, and beheld the redoubtable Director, mounted on an elephant and accompanied by three armed guards. What his thought processes were when he beheld me on the ground with the lame tigress standing in front I am unable to guess but, as she fled on three legs, he urged the elephant he was mounted on in pursuit. However, I was able to dissuade him, but the next day and every day thereafter he took to visiting the cave, ostensibly to demonstrate his concern for the wounded animal, but really to show her to his guests, until she got so alarmed that she abandoned her shelter. When a vet finally came to have a look, she was no longer visible.

I became increasingly anxious as the monsoon approached, for I realized that with the outbreak of the rains I would lose touch; the shallow water which afforded her relief would be in spate and, whereas I had hitherto known where to contact her, I would find it increasingly difficult to locate her in case any positive steps were to be taken towards a rescue operation. Despite entreaties to the Director who promised action, no positive steps were taken. I even wrote to the Prime Minister, Rajiv Gandhi, who was also the Chairman of the Indian Board for Wildlife, but he was possibly too preoccupied to bother to reply. Meanwhile, the monsoons broke, fortunately somewhat later than usual, allowing the young tigress a further respite. But once the waters rose to flood-level proportions, I lost touch though I continued my efforts to maintain contact by the tethering of bait.

Lest I be accused of the cruel practice of tying bait, may I assure my readers that the insensitive buffaloes do not live in fear awaiting death, but are tranquil even on the approach of the predator. The terror of the animal as it is dragged and trussed in the blood-soaked abattoir for human consumption is really much greater. The expedition with which the tiger dispatches his victim is at considerable odds with invocation of the name of the almighty three times, often with the accompaniment of the use of a blunt knife to sever the jugular. I therefore consider that the cause was a worthy one, and that I was entirely justified in trying to feed the afflicted tigress.

Another complication now arose, when the Male Cub by the first family took to appropriating the kill as well as guarding it, and though Tara and the other cub shared the kills, the Lame Cub was apprehensive. One morning my tracker came upon the Male Cub feeding while the Lame One sat watching 50 metres away. On a night when Tara was hunting elsewhere the Lame Cub came upon a tethered bait and clawed it to death with her left forepaw. This in itself was a great effort, as the buffalo was a large one, but she was not allowed to feed on the fruits of her efforts, and the next night the Male Cub arrived to pull the kill into cover.

Overcome by hunger the Lame Cub leapt over the 5½-foot wall of a railway pointsman, and killed three goats tethered inside. Alarmed by human shouts and the passage of a railway train, she performed the astonishing feat in her maimed condition of leaping a 7½-foot wall to safety, and starvation. The next night, overcome by ravenous hunger, she appeared near the elephant shed of the Park and chewed the arm of an old woman who was sleeping outside because of the heat, and mauled a cow.

The danger was now too close for comfort, and the Director who had resisted and postponed all my efforts to have the young tigress medically examined took immediate action, for the place of occurrence was hardly one hundred metres from where he lived. A drop cage was set up and baited at a convenient site, which the tigress entered willingly enough in her starving condition. She was sent to the Lucknow Zoo and labelled as 'Suheli, the Maneating Tigress', with the same legerdemain which had converted a captured tiger into a tigress. The Zoo vet who examined her multiple wounds, which were all the way down her right forearm, was of the opinion that gunshot wounds inflicted by a poacher had incapacitated her. Thanks to the delay of five months in providing treatment, with osteo myelitis a sinus had developed and a bone graft was the only cure. As I watched her treatment, no sooner was the suppurating wound cured at one point of her forearm than it broke out at another place on the arm.

I wrote to the Secretary of the Indian Board for Wildlife suggesting an X-ray to determine whether it would be possible to aim at Suhelis release at some conceivable time, but the State authorities were against that possibility. They claimed that she would be unable to fend for herself, and a bone graft was not possible, what with the complete non-availability of replacement grafts. I suggested that if she were to be caged, I should be allowed the privilege of looking after her, and would arrange for the construction of a spacious cage in the forest. But this suggestion did not find favour, presumably because the authorities did not want a backlash which would claim the existence of Tara, the fifth generation zoo-born tigress who returned to free living. Meanwhile, Suheli the Maneater, whose name I wish to clear, was transferred to the Delhi Zoo where she lives, while Tara her mother runs her fifteenth year in the Dudhwa National Park.

13 The Maneater of Salukapur

THE forest rest house of Salukapur is situated in the centre of the southern boundary of the Dudhwa National Park. An escarpment runs along the entire length and separates the hardwood and valuable Sal from the grasslands created over the millennia by the fluctuations of the unstable Sharda river. The rest house overlooks a savannah of coarse grasses limited by the Soheli river, which forms the physical boundary of the Park. Sloughs and marshes left by the drain-off of the flood waters keep the area lush and damp, with heavy outcrops of grass and narkul.

The rest houses served as halting stations chiefly for inspecting officers of the Forest Department, as most road surfaces were once uneven, badly maintained and largely unmetalled, and overnight halts were essential for supervision as well as convenience. Also, it was mandatory for the British serving officer to spend nine months in the field in areas of his jurisdiction, and a variety of interests in the out-doors made the appointment of a Forest Officer a prize posting. Nowadays, with improved transport facilities, lack of favoured recreational conditions, and the frequent demands of political bosses for their presence, these rest houses are no longer used by Indian touring officers, and have largely fallen into a state of disrepair.

The first to go was the Forest Lodge of Kiratpur on the western boundary of the Park. It was abandoned because it was reputed to be haunted. Legend relates that a young officer was so overwhelmed by the conditions of solitude that he took to the bottle and, after a particularly thick night, looked into a pair of bloodshot eyes peering over his shoulder into his shaving mirror in the morning. Whatever the reason, Kiratpur was knocked down and ceased to exist as a rest house. Other lodges are in disuse, but one is utilized as the headquarters for the Rhino Reintroduction Project, where two males and one female from Assam and four females from Nepal have been introduced into 29 square kilometres of grassland habitat. The proposal is to introduce a maximum of thirty animals, to provide a second home for a species which is endangered throughout its global range.

At 7 p.m. on an April evening, S.D. Singh, Range Officer, South Sonaripur in the Dudhwa National Park, took off from Salukapur on his motorcycle to return to his headquarters at Sonaripur with Parmeshwar, a tractor cleaner, as pillion passenger. He was locally in charge of the Rhino Reintroduction Project and, according to the Director of the Park, had to oversee certain rostering duties at 6.30 p.m. before leaving for home. They never returned, and while the anxiety of their dependants can be imagined, for each had a wife and small daughter, no attempt at a search was made till 7.30 the next morning, though a wireless link with Salukapur existed. The motorcycle was discovered lying in a hole on the edge of the road. The headlight was still flickering dimly. By this time a large crowd had collected and most signs of the night's events obliterated.

A search by elephants revealed the body of Parmeshwar twenty-five yards to the west of the capsized motorcycle, where a tiger had seized him. Gaping wounds on the nape of his neck, from which blood had oozed out into a pool, revealed the cause of death, but the body was untouched. Blood stains twenty-five yards to the east of the road showed where the tiger had overpowered the Range Officer, after having abandoned Parmeshwar. He had dragged S.D. Singh past the dead body of his first victim into a patch of *ratwa*, where he had eaten one leg and a part of the other. The dead bodies were covered by shrouds, after having been located by the elephants and the tiger scared away by gunshot. As there was no suitable weapon in the Park, or anyone with experience to deal with the situation, I was summoned in my capacity as Honorary Wildlife Warden.

I was sitting in a hideout on the banks of the Neora, trying to take a picture of Tara, my rehabilitated tigress, who the authorities claimed had been destroyed as a maneater five years earlier, when the sad news arrived. I remember thinking that the tiger, however sinned against had done his image no good by this deliberate killing of two men seemingly secure in the protection of a noisy motor vehicle and its headlight. A possible reconstruction of events had been obscured by innumerable footprints, but it is my surmise that the Range Officer had seen the tiger on the road in the headlight, and had tried to turn around as he had done on a previous occasion, and the vehicle had fallen into the hole on the edge. Thereafter, left defenceless he and his companion panicked and ran in opposite directions, sealing their fate. The circumstances by which the tiger compounded this felony by a double slaughter will remain a mystery, and the dramatic timing of the killings a starkly poignant human tragedy. But it is likely that S.D. Singh called to Parmeshwar, and the tiger abandoned his first victim to seize the Range Officer.

The culpability of the Forest Department in this succession of distressing events is manifest throughout. Though sporadic cases of man-eating had taken place since March 1978 inside the Park and its buffer area, and though confrontations had become endemic in cultivated areas outside the Park, no rules of entry into tiger areas had been evolved by the Department to safeguard our national animal, or indeed its prospective human victims. Though traffic lights and zebra crossings inhibit road accidents at crossroads, and motorists are not penalized for running over a pedestrian advancing against a red light, lone men enter tiger habitat during hours of darkness, and the ultimate penalty is sought against the voteless tiger by the vote-seeking politician and his sycophantic executives. It is unfortunate that, though the problem is a socio-ecological one, the human element is categorized into the sufferers who live at grassroot level, and the academics in the dove-cotes of power who could not care less. Project Tiger authorities talk glibly of Multiple-Use Areas, when it is obvious that such a consummation merely provides increasing areas of confrontation, especially when viewed against the background of the decimation of prey animals by local cultivators. A Tiger Watch, which was specially recommended by an Enquiry Committee appointed in 1978 to monitor the activities of tigers that might come into conflict with human activities, did not come into being till 1983. Since then it has become a farce. Its composition was slashed by the Finance Department on grounds of economy. The new vehicle allotted to it was taken over by the parent Forest Department. Thanks to a feud between the Park Director and the Chief Wildlife Warden, the Tiger Watch which was earmarked by a government order to be under the overall charge of the Dudhwa Park Director, was taken charge of by the Chief Wildlife Warden in his faraway headquarters, and an officer with no experience of tigers or the use of firearms was put in charge of the Watch as his first posting; he was issued with a light rifle and dud ammunition and informed that he would be responsible for any further human deaths.

The Park Director must bear a share of the responsibility for the killing of his two subordinates, for the Forest Department had so emasculated Tiger Watch that it was unable to function effectively. A

male tiger had killed and devoured the wireless operator at night
outside the Sonaripur range headquarters. He was also suspected of
having killed two men outside the Park in its buffer zone. Yet the
Director sanctioned the extraction of fuel wood and thatching material in a massive operation by local settlers. The tiger killed four men
in rapid succession in this unbridled habitat intrusion. Nature had
rebelled against the invasion. But the sands were running out as the
tiger infringed man-made rules in defence of his habitat. He was now
often seen in the vicinity, and his extraordinary boldness became a
subject for comment. S.D. Singh had once earlier turned his motorcycle when seeing a tiger on the road, and the Director knew very
well that this was a man-killer indeed. Yet he did not arrange for a
change in the rostering timings, or for a vehicle to escort the Range
Officer to his home. In fact, the Director had commandeered the jeep
allotted to the Reintroduction Project for his own use.

A few days earlier I had gone with some tourists on the Sonaripur-
Salukapur road, and in the late evening we saw the tiger walking up
the road. He crouched as he saw us, but as we stopped and watched
him from about ten yards away, he rose to his feet, crossed the road
and slowly passed within five yards of us, as everyone gazed in
fascination. He sprayed a tree, and rejoined the road he had left to
avoid us. Further on, he stood erect to rake his claws against a Dhak
tree in a further release of tension and awareness. We returned to
drive past him again, where he was crouching on the side of the road,
but as we watched he once again came on to the road and sat down,
apparently waiting for us to give him the right of way. He kept gazing
upwards, and I remarked to one of our guests that he was birdwatch-
ing. However, in the light of future events and looking back on my
associations, and how my tigress used to stare into space when she
contemplated some future action, I am convinced that he was trying
to work out how he could winkle out one of the many humans
watching him for his own delectation. I think that this tiger of great
and growing confidence, familiarized by the human presence, could
well have tackled one of the numerous vehicles in which tourists
continued their unending search for the sight of a tiger. Perhaps the
episode with the motorcycle was a step in that direction.

I armed myself with a double-barrelled ·500 Express rifle made by
Westley Richards and approached the covered body of the Range
Officer on an elephant. A low growl indicated that the tiger had
returned to his kill; but in spite of pressurizing, he refused to leave
the heavy cover. After much pursuit he crossed through a narrow
neck of grass and I took a shot at his striped pelage. He grunted to

the shot, and I later discovered he had fractured his pelvis. After a further chase my second shot broke his shoulder, and a third took him low in the neck. His adrenalin glands were now working full speed, and though the third bullet momentarily stunned him, he was up again as I hesitated over firing a fourth shot, and took cover in another patch of tall grass.

While I had been hunting the tiger, the Director had been away on some errand of his own, and he only arrived when we were about to defer the search for a few hours. However, he was determined to be a part of the act, and climbed up beside me on the elephant, and insisted on following the tiger into some thick grass. He had long since returned the Magnum with the broken catch with which he had shot the Median tigress, but he fired off a cartridge into the grass. The dying animal charged out and mauled the elephant. But this was the last flicker, and we found him dead on our return. The Director refused to allow anyone to take pictures, as he claimed that the tiger had not been declared a maneater, and no one had been specifically designated to destroy him. Deferring to my knowledge of English he gave an interview to a Hindi newspaper, in which he stated that even an 'accomplished hunter' such as I had not been able to kill the erring tiger, which had attacked the elephant, and that he had fallen off but quickly recovered to finish off the charging beast. To my question as to why he had given a false statement, he appeared offended, and said he could not be responsible for what news correspondents put out.

The tiger was of average size, and with no visible infirmities. The post mortem revealed no reasons as to why he had become a maneater; however, he was not in good condition, and weighed barely 350 pounds. I estimated his age at between ten to twelve years. The fact that he had only eaten one leg and a portion of the other from his kills during twelve hours revealed that his appetite was not in keeping with the prodigious hunger of other able-bodied and healthy conspecifics. Why he had turned into a maneater, and what physiological and psychological imperatives had urged him to this fateful and unnatural way of life will never be determined, but we must examine afresh the reasons for these so-called aberrations. The causes which applied in the days of the legendary hunter of maneaters, Jim Corbett, do not apply in their entirety now. The animals which he destroyed were handicapped by age or wounds. The present-day tigers who have taken to such a habit are mainly young and healthy.

14 Splay Toes –
Almost a Maneater

IN October 1987 a line of seven buffalo carts wended their way along the metalled road to Palia, past National Park Headquarters at Dudhwa. They were loaded with paddy which had been traded for red chillies with the Tharus living on the Nepal border. Suddenly a tiger rushed out of the undergrowth, wrenched a buffalo yoked to the last cart out of its harness, and pulled it down the embankment into the dense grass by the side of the road. The other buffalo panicked and fled, leaving the loaded and derelict cart on the road. News of the assault spread like wildfire, and trucks and buses plying the highway streaked past blowing their horns at full blast.

Four days later I went to investigate. Deciduous leaf litter lay thick on the slopes of the embankment and, as I slithered down the slippery incline, the tiger charged out of the undergrowth with bellowing grunts, to be turned away, as I recovered sufficiently to wave my stick and shout. But he came on again, his snarling mouth agape, devoid of canines. A travesty of a noble predator, and our national animal. Four times the hungry tiger repeated this demonstration, for he still had enough armament to have killed me each time, and eaten me as well. For four days he had sat guarding his kill, unable to penetrate the tough hide without his canines. Starving, and suffering from the considerable stress of trucks and buses speeding past and blowing their hooters loudly, he was sufficiently upset to launch these demonstrations in defence of his prey, yet he refrained from wiping me out of the way.

Tigresses are far more stable in range occupations than tigers. This is possibly because of the stronger territorial instinct of the male, induced by a natural mating urge which required a larger range encompassing that of a number of females; and a greater flux, as dominance factors come into play. Tara had been on the Tiger Haven range as a wild tigress since 1978, and by 1989 several dominant tigers—Old Crooked Foot, Long Toes, Tara's Male, the Male Cub and Splay Toes had come and gone. In 1987, Tara's Male disappeared with the monsoon, and the Male Cub, who was Tara's offspring by Tara's Male, also vanished some time later.

During September 1987 a strange tiger appeared on the range with a diagnostically splayed toe on either forepaw. I originally thought that this might be Tara's Male with a distortion of age on either paw, but these tracks were much smaller than the great pugs of the father figure, and I concluded that an outward swagger as the tiger walked was responsible for his distinctive pugmarks. I named him Splay Toes. Tara at this time was bringing up two cubs of her third family, and by the way he associated with them at kills, it appeared that he was a sibling from a previous one.

In early December another tiger hobbled across the western boundary of Tiger Haven at mid-day and entered a patch of sugarcane. At night a tiger, presumably Splay Toes, called to the east, for tigers appear to become aware of the presence of other conspecifics by some form of esoteric telecommunication, and the lame tiger turned west to walk past Tiger Haven, and into the Spillway Copse where I had often seen him while he shared the range with his father. He rested there for a week and then appeared in the morning at a kill, which Splay Toes was sharing with Tara and her family. He scavenged from the remains, crossed the Neora river, and disappeared into cover, but not before I had the mortification of recognizing Tara's Male Cub of her first family in that emaciated feline, his right foreleg swollen to twice its normal dimension dangling by his side, and a wound above his wrist by a poacher's bullet.

I reported the appearance of this wounded tiger to Tiger Watch. I also sought the permission of the Park Director to bait this particular tiger in order to immobilize him and examine his wound. The Director accorded his permission, and a special tracker from Tiger Watch was deputed to assist in the operation. However, Departmental interest evaporated at this stage, the tracker simulated illness and returned to his headquarters.

In the hope that the lame cub would make a kill, I tied out a bait opposite the double-storeyed machan which I had constructed about twenty-five years earlier to observe wildlife. However, Splay Toes took the bait, and an angling gash across his nostrils in the morning confirmed that a confrontation had taken place. The afflicted Male Cub had then disappeared up the escarpment, a fugitive in the range where he had been born a scant five years ago. Three months later at evenfall, across the immensity of space from the west there floated the cadence of a spacing call. It faded away only to rise in a commanding paean. From the east Splay Toes, alerted by the calls, approached, growling menacingly, and at dusk there was a brief skirmish over possession of a kill. All night the heavily armed felines fed alternately on the carcass without inflicting injury on each other. In the morning, as a companion and I approached to inspect the site, with thunderous roars the tigers joined in brief but ferocious combat. As the heavy grasses bulged and heaved during the fracas, we stood not upon the order of our going! They broke off, and Splay Toes retired, growling loudly, and soon a spacing call drifted in from the west. The Male Cub fed noisily before departing south, a grotesquely twisted pugmark proof that, after a convalescence, he had returned, albeit briefly, to the range. It also illustrates that a familial recognition will establish a dominance relationship among those lethal predators, in lieu of a possible internecine confrontation. However, the Male Cub moved out, and Splay Toes continued in the Tiger Haven range with Tara and her cubs.

In May 1988 a moaning call from the east, in what I knew as the Mating Copse, drew my attention to the fact that a possible mating was about to occur: the patent vocalizations were taking place—the moaning approach of the tiger, and the snarling riposte of the tigress. But the soundings did not appear purposeful enough, and they were moving about and were not static as in resolute matings. In the morning I identified the two animals as Tara and Splay Toes by their pugs on the sandy bank of the river, but the peripatetic vocalizations continued and it seemed that, though Tara was in season, Splay Toes had not attained the dominance required for a meaningful mating, either because of his lineal relationship, or his age. They were together for another day, and parted soon after. Tara did not mate till 1989.

Just after the monsoon a tiger appeared on the Dudhwa-Palia highway. He accidentally killed a man when he charged two bullocks that were being herded. He then attacked a pony cart and knocked it off the embankment. Appalled by the circumstances of the attacks, he disappeared without following up his advantage. He continued his assaults on domestic stock which grazed inside the buffer area of the Park. Complicated by his inability to feed, I investigated this phenomenon, and discovered to my dismay that this was Splay Toes. I reported the matter to the Park Director, and the Assistant Conservator in charge of Tiger Watch. As a result, a ludicrous charade was

initiated, and a number of untrained graduates, who had been en-
listed as trackers, were detailed to monitor the tiger's movements.
Visits to the Park by the Director's guests, mounted on elephants,
were stepped up as everyone wanted to glimpse the elusive feline.

The night of 7–8 November was full moon, and the dirt track
leading to Tiger Haven gleamed like two pale ribbons. The white coat
of my goat, Aboubakr, shimmered in the moonlight as Splay Toes
walked towards the garage where the goat was tethered to a bullock
cart. Aboubakr had come to me as a bait in 1973 to locate Prince, my
leopard who had opted for freedom earlier that year. But though he
was often tethered in the forest to attract the leopard by his vaunted
bleating, he escaped the attention not only of Prince but that of
Prince's future consort, Harriet, and ultimately of Tara despite his
strong goat smell, which he periodically augmented by his acrobatic
ability to urinate on his head. When he was tied in the forest, instead
of bleating his heart out to attract the predators, he would curl up and
go to sleep until roused from his slumbers by the concealed observer
in various stages of cramp and frustration. No cat had thus far discovered the treat in store for it, and Aboubakr had evaded his destiny
and become instead a mascot at Tiger Haven.

On that fateful night of the full moon when Splay Toes grabbed
Aboubakr from his refuge, he pulled the rubber-tyred cart to which
the goat was tethered down a slope. As the cart rolled on to him, the
tiger let out a loud roar and fled, but the goat was dead by the time
we got to him. Aboubakr had lived out his life and belatedly fulfilled
his destiny. We untethered the offending cart, and tied the dead
animal to a tree. But Splay Toes returned later to pull the goat into
some heavy grass.

Aboubakr had seemed a rather unattractive animal to me in his
earlier days, chiefly because of his salacious approaches to other
animate entities regardless of their sex or species. He even gave the
impression that a predator would have to get past his sexual advances; but I had got quite fond of him, and as his sex-motivated sallies
became restricted with advancing years he acquired an expression of
infinite wisdom. Besides, one could not but admire him for joining in
battle with full-grown buffaloes, or his tenacious hold on life in one
of his later illnesses when, after a life-restoring injection from the vet,
he launched a powerful butt at him, only to fall over again. Thus,
when the tiger removed the old goat I became obsessed with according his remains the honour of a burial in my animal cemetery and,
without due consideration, sent my tracker to rescue what was left.
However, Splay Toes had other ideas, and sprang upon him and

mauled his arm despite our shouts. We only found Aboubakr's horns and a few vertebrae for interment.

Having at last had a viable meal, the tiger started visiting my premises on a regular basis, and we would find his distinctive pugs on irrigation channels and in the vegetable garden. This development was alarming to say the least. It was by now fairly obvious that the tiger was afflicted in some way and was unable to utilize prey with tough hides; the fact that he appreciated more pliable flesh and visited the site of his windfall regularly, made it almost certain that, with growing hunger, my vulnerable staff whose quarters were within a few yards of where he visited, would be next on the list. As the Park authorities were taking no action, I decided that I must divert the tiger's attention, as well as discover what affliction prevented him from making a meal of the animals he was able to kill. I therefore tethered a buffalo bait opposite the double-storeyed machan. I also installed lighting arrangements, controlled by a rheostat, to observe the tiger during the process of feeding. Splay Toes killed the bait that night, and my visit in the morning revealed the dead animal with four bruises on its throat, and the power in his canineless jaws which had strangulated the buffalo. He then retired to a patch of grass across the river from where he would growl when he heard visitors at his kill.

That night by fortuitous chance Tara and her cubs came to open the kill, and it must have been with an extraordinary sense of relief that Splay Toes was able to share the contents of his kill with his mother and other siblings. I was also able to observe that he had a third of a canine left, probably caused by the explosion of an 'infernal device' placed in his kill of domestic stock as a retaliatory measure by the owner. The next kill Splay Toes made was dispatched in similar fashion, but Tara was wandering elsewhere and did not arrive to open the kill, and Splay Toes sat guarding it and scowling at alighting vultures. I therefore saw no alternative but to disembowel the carcass, and went with my tracker the next morning to do so. However, the tiger was still sitting beside the kill instead of retiring to the grass patch, and we passed within five yards of him. I verily believe he would not have tried to molest us, for we were acquaintances who occupied the same range, and had fed him; but I let off a gun shot in the air, and after he fled in alarm we went and disembowelled the kill. I had the satisfaction of seeing him feed the next morning. He even abandoned the kill on my approach instead of demonstrating, as he did in the case of the cart buffalo where he had been upset by noisy traffic.

I reported my observations to the Park Director, and took the Park

Warden and the officer in charge of Tiger Watch to see the site of the kill, from where I had suggested that the afflicted tiger be baited with a view to immobilizing him, and either destroyed or sent to a zoo. I had a meeting with the Park Director and Park Warden on 4 and 5 December, and the former wrote to me on 8 December confirming that it was within his knowledge that I had provided a bait for the tiger with the blown-out canines, and that the animal was able to kill but not open the carcass until a tigress did it for him. The Director also sought my advice on the steps to be taken to prevent the tiger from becoming a maneater. However, when I showed him a photograph of the canineless Splay Toes he pushed it away with the remark that processes of nature must take their course. He had no answer to my query whether nature had put a bomb in the kill.

On 17 December, guided by the Park Warden and another person connected with Tiger Watch, the Director raided the kill site with a posse of armed guards and three elephants. He destroyed the double-storeyed machan and confiscated the equipment with which I had monitored the tiger; he then filed a prosecution case against me for baiting tigers to show tourists. He demolished a bridge over the Neora that had been constructed by the Forest Department connecting them to a stronghold for the swampdeer and for which I had given the Department right of way through my land. He forbade my entry into the Park, though I was an Honorary Wildlife Warden appointed by the Government, and erected an electric fence to keep me out, though that meant cutting wildlife off from a permanent source of water.

It is difficult to imagine such a change of attitude taking place within a period of ten days, unless the circumstances are related. The Park staff had been making money by encouraging the adjacent population to extract timber from the forest by payment of a subvention, and selling it in the open market. Such extraction was against the provisions of the Indian Wildlife (Protection) Act of 1972. The plunder increased rapidly, and poaching, encouraged by those illegal activities, spread. A tiger killed four people who had intruded in his habitat, and was promptly declared a maneater.

Unable to countenance such robbery, I applied for a Stay Order from the High Court against the illicit extraction of wood from the Park, which was granted. Such an action also put the kybosh on the expectation of votes by the Chief Minister of Uttar Pradesh, who had his weather eye on the coming election, for the local populace threatened to vote for another party. His ire knew no bounds, and inspite of my entertaining him when he came to Dudhwa, he took away Wildlife from the Forest Portfolio, put it under himself, transferred the incumbent Director (and a good friend of mine) and posted a junior with a previous bad record to deal with my recalcitrance, which he did as related.

Beset by my own immediate problems of legal action against me, I was unable to feed Splay Toes. Weighted by his physical infirmities, yet aided by the charity which is in nature, he lingered briefly on the Tiger Haven range until, shrouded in the mantle of his regal past, he faded into oblivion. Thus ended the tragic episode of Splay Toes. Yet nemesis stalks both ways; the Chief Minister had a heart failure in a foreign country, and his party lost at the hustings.

The above account is not that of a maneater, but about one which should have become that because of his man-made affliction. He accidently killed a man, mauled another, and could have slain others had he been inclined that way. He suffered greatly, but despite sitting beside his kill for four days without being able to feed, he did not attack another human.

15 The Maneater of Banga Jhala

THE forest hamlet of Garjia, on the west bank of the river Kosi, lies just outside the boundary of the Corbett National Park. Across the river from Garjia, and connected to it by footpaths, are the village of Chopra and two others, all illegal encroachments into the forest made by villagers with the encouragement of unscrupulous local politicians. The area of wild, wooded country east of the river is known as Banga Jhala.

Short cuts between the hamlets, constantly used by villagers, run through forest of Sal and lantana. With the lantana, plenty of water and a good supply of prey animals (chiefly sambar, chital and wild boar), Banga Jhala is a perfect area for tigers—or would be, were it not for the human interlopers. Late in the evening of 21 March 1979, two villagers who had been to collect their weekly rations in Garjia were returning home to Chopra with a pack horse. Attracted by the animal's neighing, and disregarding the chatter of human voices which he had no doubt heard on numerous occasions as people passed through his domain, a tiger launched an attack on the horse as it came near a dense lantana thicket. It is not clear whether anyone was astride, but the tiger missed the horse, which bolted, and in the ensuing mêlée one of the men was knocked down and killed.

Since tigers do not normally prey on humans, whom they regard as an alien species, I presume that the attacker initially baulked at the strange carcass which he had got by accident, but that hunger and the confidence of being a big male then overcame his hesitation, and he had his first human meal.

Naturally the death created panic in the area; but as weeks went by with no further attack, fear gradually died down, and the incident was almost forgotten. Then, twenty-two months later, another man, also from Chopra, was taken—this time an employee of the Forest Department who set out alone as dawn was breaking on 19 January 1981 to mark stumps on a site where contractors were felling timber. This time the tiger made a deliberate kill though, once again, the exact circumstances of the attack are not known. It may be that the man had squatted down behind a bush to relieve himself, and that the tiger sprang on mistaking him for a four-legged animal. Six months later, on 25 June, a third man, a lone honey collector, was also eaten, only fifty yards from where the second incident had taken place.

Pugmark tracings confirmed that all three kills were the work of the same big male. Of course, the blame for the deaths was placed on Project Tiger, the international scheme launched in 1972 by India and other nations for saving the tiger from extinction. Although the Corbett National Park had existed since 1935, new wildlife reserves had been created as part of the Project, and the population of tigers had stabilized, perhaps even increased. Now, people said, it was because their numbers had reached dangerous proportions that the man-eating had started. It was certainly true that tigers were living in the Banga Jhala buffer zone of forest outside the park.

The villagers went to their local politician, who happened to be a member of the national government, and because he was a powerful man he was able to get the tiger officially declared a maneater without delay. In other areas an attempt might well have been made to shoot the animal, but here, the Field Director of the Park had at least accepted my contention that alleged maneaters should not be destroyed out of hand. He did not, however, agree with my suggestion that the tiger should be transferred to some more suitable area and given another chance there; rather, he planned, if he could catch it live, to put it into a zoo.

But in 1981 India lacked both the equipment for darting tigers, and the experience of using it. The result was that when the Field Director and a young research assistant with no field experience set out to capture the Maneater of Banga Jhala, they were able to procure only one serviceable radio dart, and no antidote. Soon, after a fruitless wait for the tiger, they compounded their difficulties by irresponsibly firing off their single projectile at a female sambar, which fortunately they missed. Their only hope now was to try to trap the tiger, and for this they got hold of a portable steel cage, which they camouflaged with vegetation and placed close to a site on which buffaloes had been tethered as baits. After the tiger had made a few kills, they laid a trail by dragging the remains of a dead bait to the cage and leaving it inside the drop-gate over the entrance. That night the tiger came, but after he had half-entered the cage he became alarmed and withdrew.

By then the operation had been made even more difficult by heavy monsoon rain. The Kosi and all the local streams were in spate, and flood water lay everywhere. It was decided that if the next attempt failed, the whole campaign would have to be abandoned until the rains and floods had subsided. Another adverse factor was that the tiger had become exceedingly wary as a result of continuous pursuit. Yet that very night, impelled by twenty-four hours of hunger, he sealed his own fate by stepping into the cage which caused the door to drop behind him.

Next morning the Field Director and his entourage had already loaded their luggage into a waiting car and were on the point of departure when a radio message arrived from the reconnaissance party to say that the tiger was in the trap. As can be imagined, excitement and elation swept through the camp, and everyone hastened to the scene of action.

The Field Director himself has given a vivid description of the scene: as they drew near the cage, he writes, an eerie hush prevailed over the area. No birds called, and even the ever-vociferous cicadas had fallen silent. Nothing could be seen of the heavily-camouflaged cage except the entrance, which by then was closed with a gate of steel bars.

Suddenly, at the approach of the domestic elephants with their human riders, there was an immense explosion of roars as the concealed tiger hurled himself towards his tormentors and the massive cage shook under the onslaught. The elephants trumpeted and panicked, and for a few moments pandemonium reigned. Once their mounts were back under control, the onlookers gathered round the cage, from which the tiger glared and snarled at his enemies.

Already his face and paws were a bloody mess of bruises and contusions, and in his struggle to free himself he had also smashed his nose. To save him from further injury it was decided to sedate him; but this was less simple than it seemed for his adrenal glands were in full production, and several extra doses of drugs were needed to knock him out. At last, by 3 p.m., he had been rendered unconscious.

The raging dynamo of a few minutes before now lay inert in the cage; but as the Field Director surveyed him, along with his research assistant and Brijendra Singh, a young volunteer conservationist and wildlife photographer who had come down from Delhi to help, the first qualms of conscience appear to have assailed them. Their flush of euphoria at having humbled the mighty carnivore quickly abated to be replaced by the remorse which comes to anyone with human feelings who has destroyed a symbol.

Now that they had done it, they made hectic arrangements to convey the tiger to Lucknow Zoo as quickly as possible. Because of the difficulty of fording the flooded rivers, it was not until the next afternoon that the truck carrying the still partially-sedated animal reached the zoo.

By then the tiger had spent forty hours in the trap, along with the remains of the rotting kill, which was full of maggots. His wounds had become infected, and he was induced to enter a squeeze cage so that his lacerated face and broken nose could be treated. Then for two days he touched neither food nor water. Yet soon he made an attempt to regain his freedom: at night, finding that the thick iron sheet which lined the floor of his prison was loose at one end, he prised it up with his paws and powerful jaws and tore it to shreds as though it were a piece of tinfoil.

Spattered with blood from his injured paws and belly, which had been ripped by the strips of torn-up iron, he was frantically working on the more vulnerable wooden planks underneath when the zoo staff discovered him making his bid for liberty. Had he escaped, it is anyone's guess what havoc he would have wreaked before nemesis finally overtook him or he found temporary refuge in some outlying piece of forest, for there was no habitat suitable for a tiger anywhere near the zoo. As it was, he was immediately transferred to another cage, in which he seized a piece of angle iron and bent it double with his teeth, breaking one of his canines in the process. By now all his wounds were full of maggots.

In a somewhat premature report published in August 1981, 'A Complete Account of the First Successful Live Capture of a Free-Ranging, Man-Eating Tiger', the Field Director expressed the hope that 'Banga' would gradually become reconciled to the restrictions of his new existence. But it was not to be. Six months later the tiger made his final bid for freedom. His spirit broken by imprisonment and the battering he had received, he played his last card by dying, unobserved, in his cage. A post mortem pronounced the cause of death as an infestation of tapeworms. This is a common ailment among wild tigers—perhaps because they sometimes eat putrescent flesh; but they normally recover quickly.

Whatever the immediate cause of the prisoner's demise, I am sure he would soon have died anyway, for it is my firm belief that a tiger which has lived wild and enjoyed the freedom of a large range cannot be expected to survive in captivity. There is no record of a tiger captured as an adult having lived for any length of time in captivity. To deny a wild creature its freedom is a crime against the laws of nature—and to believe anything else is futile self-deception.

The key question posed by the distressing incident was this: Should the tiger have been officially declared a maneater in the first place? According to the criteria laid down by that great hunter-naturalist Jim Corbett, he should not have. Corbett maintained that a tiger should be classed as a maneater only if it had been shown that he sought human flesh compulsively (the Champawat and Panar maneaters, for instance, killed 836 known humans). The Banga Jhala tiger never did this. He killed three men in twenty-eight months; the first died by accident, and the other two were on their own in the forest where no one had any business to go alone.

Whose fault was it that they died? The tiger had long since been declared India's national animal and strenuous efforts had been made to preserve it. Everyone concerned with the welfare of tigers had anticipated that, once the animals were fully protected, they would spill over from Corbett Park and colonize buffer areas of forest—exactly what happened at Banga Jhala. There, this tiger's legitimate home had been encroached upon by illegal human habitation, and the wild-pig and deer on which he lived gunned down by crop-protection firearms. Humans had fallen into the habit of passing through the forest and lantana thickets in which he lived, never acknowledging that they were trespassers in tiger territory.

The fiasco of Banga Jhala precisely illustrates in microcosm the great problem which is the theme of this book. Can a 'Third-World' democracy, with its population spiralling out of control towards the appalling figure of one billion people, afford living space to the greatest predator on earth? Or will the huge effort of Project Tiger prove no more than a delaying action, a brief pause in the tiger's march towards extinction?

16 Sheroo

BEFORE a ban was imposed in India and Nepal on tiger shooting, tigers were lured to their destruction by the tethering of buffalo bait in areas they were likely to pass during their night-time perambulations in search of prey, and which also had suitable cover where they could lie up during the day; they would then be driven out by elephants or men, to be shot from strategically placed machans by shikaris armed with sophisticated rifles. In Nepal, as has already been described, the tigers were surrounded by elephants and, in a later development, by strips of white cloth which they hesitated to cross, and were gunned down by trained, skirmishing elephants, with mounted shikaris.

In 1973 Project Tiger was launched in Corbett National Park under the sponsorship of Mrs Indira Gandhi, and the recommendation of the WWF. Originally nine areas were selected, and by 1991 this had reached eighteen. Baiting, however, continued as a means to display the tiger to tourists, who have now taken the place of shikaris. In spite of many other forms of spectacular wildlife, the intrinsic tourist value of the tiger occupies a unique focal point for tourism, and tourists unable to view a tiger feel they have missed out on the purpose of their visit. It is like arriving in Agra, only to find the Taj Mahal covered by fog.

However, tourism has arrived too late in India to lay claim to saving its wildlife. Africa, with its display in the shop window, and wildlife as its foreign exchange earner, can afford to have parks of the size of Selous in Tanzania of 21,000 square miles, Kafue in Zimbabwe of 12,500 and Tsavo in Kenya of 8,000. India, with its human population already established and its closed habitat for wildlife, makes do with 525 square kilometres in Corbett, and even 105 square kilometres as in Bandavgarh. But wildlife in both India and Africa is endangered, even if for different reasons: in India, by habitat destruction and degradation, and in Africa by commercial poaching as a billion-dollar industry, which has decimated the rhino and the elephant.

Baiting was finally discontinued in India in 1982. The practice was regarded by Mrs Gandhi as cruel and inhuman, but as I said to her, 'Madam, your butcher kills for you, and he does so in a vastly more inhuman fashion than the tiger'. Baiting, though ultimately an unnecessary and unnatural practice in wildlife management, has a definite use for the wildlife manager in the present context. Baiting may be used as a temporary source of easing the predation pressure on areas with limited prey populations, and encouraging the increase of predator populations to optimum capacity. It may also be used for scientific studies, for the location of aberrant predators, and for the assistance of ailing or gravid tigers in times of need, bearing in mind the present pressure on habitat areas.

The Corbett National Park, unlike the Dudhwa Park has a wide buffer zone which should be able to absorb the spillover of tigers claimed by the breeding success in the Reserve, but cases of man-eating have occurred, and three of them have been powerful and dominant animals who have behaved aberrantly thanks to excessive human incitement, though Corbett is well stocked with prey. I give brief accounts of the incarceration of the three tigers—Banga, Sheroo and Dhitoo, for it gave the Director of the Reserve satisfaction in identifying with his victims for imprisonment and slow death, while functioning as Judge and Jury.

Sheroo, named as such by the original Director of the Tiger Reserve who admired the machismo of this large tiger, was extensively baited as a tourist attraction. Once located he was relentlessly pursued by elephants, beyond the reasonable viewing requirements of tourists. As I remarked on one occasion, the pursuit was like the Ring Method of Nepal when the chase only ended with the destruction of the tiger. In addition, the Director used to hurl abuse at Sheroo at the top of his voice, presumably to boost his own masculine image, as well as to display his familiarity with an animal whom people had crossed continents to see.

Tigers are highly intelligent animals, conscious of their unassailable position in the comity of jungle denizens, and have a dignity which should not be denigrated. There is no doubt that Sheroo resented the chivvying by elephants he was compelled to undergo, and the imaginative abuse he was subjected to by the Director and his cohorts. In correspondence which I had with the Director he insisted that Sheroo's aggression was mainly directed towards elephants and the handlers. Though I have only limited experience of the Corbett Park, I am convinced by my own experience that the tiger's resentment was caused by the unrelenting pursuit he was subjected to; finding the pachyderms out of his prey range, he reacted towards the fodder cutters who accompanied the elephant, usually alone.

Sheroo first displayed signs of aggressive behaviour during the early months of 1982. He occupied the Chuisoti beat where he was chiefly baited, and one day Brijendra Singh went to sit up on a machan where a bait had been killed, hoping to take some cine pictures. He was duly put up on the machan, and the elephant left the scene with everyone talking loudly to give the impression that they had all gone. In the mean time a strange sound was heard, as if the tiger was grinding his teeth in anger; he was also shaking a bush behind which he stood in order to watch what was happening. Tigers have no lateral movement of their jaws, and cannot grind their teeth in rage, but Sheroo was undoubtedly displaying anger as he launched a vicious charge at Brijendra the next moment, which brought him to within a couple of feet of the machan. Brijendra spent a fearful night in the machan, from where he was rescued in the morning. In the mean time Sheroo bit through the nylon rope with which the bait was tethered, though tigers usually try to break the rope, and dragged the kill into cover.

In April 1982 Mahesh Howard, a fodder cutter for one of the Park elephants, went into the forest with his charge. According to the Director, he located Sheroo and climbed a tree, from where he abused the tiger according to the current practice in the Reserve, and hurled missiles which he broke off the tree-top, thereby irritating Sheroo, who lay in wait; Sheroo grabbed Howard as he descended from the tree, and ate him. However, the tiger was given the benefit of the doubt, as Howard was inclined to be cocky, and the Director was convinced that he had provoked the tiger.

Two years later another fodder cutter, one Subedar Ali, went out alone with his elephant and started cutting branches within about two hundred and fifty yards from the previous accident. While he was descending from the tree he was pulled down from a height of twelve feet and mauled. The Director was culpable to the extent that, though he insisted that Sheroo was liable to attack fodder cutters, he did not insist that the *Filwan* should also accompany the elephant when it went out to gather fodder. Subedar Ali was a man of puny physique, he weighed about 120 pounds, but insisted that when the tiger pulled him down and was about to kill, with a hardihood born of desperation he caught hold of the tiger's tongue, poked his eye, and finally bit him on the nose. However, on hearing Subedar's yells another elephant arrived on the scene and the tiger moved away. Subedar Ali had been mauled on the scalp, but was able to climb on to his elephant and return to headquarters. He was taken to the Park Headquarters in Ramnagar, where the doctor said he did not have the instruments to put stitches in the man's scalp. He was then taken to Kashipur where the doctor in the hospital sewed up his scalp. Brijendra Singh, an honorary wildlife warden and a great well wisher of the Reserve, took him in to his home in Delhi and after a special dispensation from Rajiv Gandhi, whose school-fellow Brijendra had been, Subedar was taken to the All India Institute of Medical Sciences. He was discharged from there with the remark that the wounds were not serious enough to warrant admission to a hospital which had a long waiting list. However, Subedar Ali was looked after with great dedication by Brijendra and his wife Dawn, and he ultimately recovered, though he nearly died when the stitches went septic. Sheroo was blamed for the mauling, though there was a strong suspicion that the mauling had been done by a tigress with two cubs in the vicinity, and who had pulled the man off the tree in a case of mistaken identity; she abandoned him when she realized what she had caught. I wrote to the Director that a large and determined tiger like Sheroo, who weighed 500 pounds plus, would not inflict superficial wounds on a puny man, and then back off. I also pointed out that the quality of stitches put into Subedar Ali's head, which nearly cost him his life when they suppurated, was reprehensible.

However, goaded by the Chief Minister, in whose constituency Corbett Park happened to be situated, Sheroo was captured and sent to the Kanpur Zoo where he ekes out his declining years with three of his canines fractured and the dubious satisfaction of having an inbred white tigress as his companion. An acrimonious argument started with the Director in which I accused him of irresponsibility in capturing a tiger on little evidence. I also suggested that Sheroo should be euthanized. He accused me of 'inhumanity' in making this recommendation.

Another male tiger was captured and also sent to the Kanpur Zoo after David Hunt, an ornithologist who had blundered on a tigress and cubs while following a rare owl, had been killed. The male, Dhitoo, was captured after a Nepalese had been killed on entering the forest by himself in the late evening to gather wood.

17 The Twilight Years

MY final chapter may seem irrelevant as it has nothing to do with maneaters. Yet the entire argument against a hand-reared reintroduction is that the great predators lose their inborn fear of man and, not having been taught the expertise of hunting by their parents, turn on the easiest prey of all. Tara, it is claimed, was shot as a maneating tigress in 1980 on 11 November for killing five humans thanks to an alleged inability to subdue virile prey.

I have refuted this fraudulent claim by asking the counter question whether Tara lived on the five humans she killed, three of whom were uneaten, for two years and ten months. I have suggested that Tara was initially dependent on the male tiger she went off with, that predators do not have to be taught the expertise of hunting, and that their phylogenetic inheritance instructs them in the procedures of killing—as it had with my Fishing Cat who came to my care as an infant and was found looking for fish in a local stream on her own compulsive volition at the age of one month. Thereafter, practise, combined with the hunger imperative and the propensity to scavenge will ensure the survival and evolution of the complete predator.

Finally, this is the culminating account of a unique experiment and a tribute to a cub tigress who came from Twycross Zoo in England and was initially accused of being a genetic cocktail of Siberian and Sumatran blood which would pollute the Indian strain. Various interested parties connived against her survival, but she lived out her allotted span on the Tiger Haven range and disappeared from it in her fifteenth year, never having infringed the rules of man during her life. Tigers are not inveterate maneaters. Once Tara opted for a nocturnal existence the human became a stranger to be avoided.

I have encountered Tara in the river at mid-day. I have come upon her with her cubs in the evening. I have walked back from the Spillway Machan at midnight. I have met her at her kill in the morning. Yet she has never made a hostile move which would merit the insinuation that surrogate parenthood leads to man-eating.

Though tradition lays down that tigers and leopards generally have smaller families in their first productions than subsequently, I have found in my limited experience that this is not necessarily a fact. Tara, my hand-reared tigress, produced a family of three in her first effort, and a succession of two thereafter, while Harriet the leopardess had two cubs, followed by the single Mameena for her second. Unfortunately, an early death robbed me of further proof as to whether fecundity might follow a certain pattern among the solitary cats.

Though I had originally adjudged the two cubs of Tara's second family as being a male and a female, I soon discovered that they were both tigresses. Also, though Tara's Male had moved out of the range, leaving it in the custody of his son, he had returned to mate with Tara once she came into season. This occurrence also gives rise to the interesting speculation as to whether it is only the dominant male on the range who is permitted to breed, and whether the female determines this eventuality and will only submit to the male if he can subdue her.

During the summer, Tara and her two cubs were often seen in the vicinity of Juliette Point, and appeared to avoid the Spillway Site, though the former precincts were more disturbed by tourists wandering about on elephants. One day, however, the reason for her preference became obvious as I sat opposite the Western Spillway and saw Tara's Male come into the water. Confident tigers spend considerable time in the water cooling off during the hot weather, and the big fellow sat on interminably. I was fascinated, yet bored by his inaction. I wanted to leave, but could not do so. Suddenly, a tiger seemingly just as large and richly coloured appeared, to sit down beside him. For some time father and son sat together: the father placid in the cooling stream, the younger tiger restive. Literature has stressed the intolerance of big males, yet here was the dominant male sharing the water with his three-year-old son. It also explained the reason why Tara avoided that particular stretch of water with her small cubs, for though the father consorted with them, she was wary of her grown-up son.

During the winter of 1985 I became obsessed by the idea of attempting to approach Tara in order to determine the degree of familiarity to which I could return. For though she had abandoned my immediate company, we occupied the same range ever since she had left.

In October of 1984 Tara lay on a log which spanned a ravine, while her cubs fed from a kill immediately underneath. I called to her as I used to while she was with me, and she moved behind cover, from where she scowled. Gradually, her expression became more serene as she listened attentively, and it occurred to me that the suggestion that after a return to the wild she would forget might be incorrect, and our occupation of the same range still suggested her recognition of a presence she had once known so well.

She continued with the rearing of her cubs, and it was not until January 1985 that I was able to attempt a further approach. I found her feeding on a kill opposite the double-storeyed machan in the morning. I called to her and, to my surprise, she looked up and took four steps towards me until she came to the stream which flowed between us. I fell silent, and she moved away into the forest, and I to Tiger Haven, for it is not correct to push familiarity with animals, and it is they who should make the first advances. As I continued my approaches to Tara it became obvious that a return to a former relationship of dependence was not going to take place, and that acceptance, tolerance, and an individual recognition would be the basis of co-existence between a species which is entirely diurnal, and an essentially nocturnal animal who could by confidence and persuasion operate during daylight hours.

Tara demonstrated her awareness by coming at night to sniff at chairs left behind hides, and by staring intently at screens from where I watched her in the water. One afternoon she came into the river. I called to her and she listened attentively as she opened and closed her mouth. She lay down on the bank and rolled over frequently. She moved closer to repeat the gesture in an overture of friendliness, which is tiger ethos and the final gesture of acceptance by an animal capable of retaliation. The next time I saw Tara feeding on a kill I called to her, and she tolerated my approach until I got within thirty yards of her, when she moved away, with a prusten, which the young tracker with me insists he heard, but which my aging faculties did not have the satisfaction of picking up.

With the arrival of the summer months, tigers orient their habits to remain within easy reach of water. One day in April 1985 I sat on a low machan on the river bank waiting for Tara to come into the water with her cubs, who I was aware were in the Spillway Copse. Suddenly there appeared, seemingly from nowhere, a little black dog, about six to eight months old. For a brief moment it stood under the machan to gaze purposefully up-stream, where there could have been a tiger kill which it might have smelt, before setting out towards the copse. During that infinitesimal moment I realized that I should have called to the dog, and that providence had sent me a replacement for the marvellous little Eelie, who had also arrived unannounced, and who for me had been the ultimate dog. However, in nature there are often no second chances, and as a shrill prolonged scream echoed from the Spillway Copse, the little black dog had fulfilled its destiny as the family of tigers grabbed it.

However, nature did offer me a second chance when I walked along the river in the morning. I was carrying a bag with some reading material—a thing which I normally do not do. Suddenly I heard a sharp hiss, and a subdued exclamation from my young tracker behind me, and saw that a spectacled cobra with its outspread hood had struck at me, and it was only the luck of having reading material in the bag which had come between my bare skin under the shorts I was wearing and the snake's venom. As it slithered away I wondered at the strangely aggressive behaviour of the cobra, and the lucky escape I had. Perhaps the cobra was guarding eggs, or newly hatched young ones.

Tara's role in protecting and feeding one of her injured cubs has been described separately in 'Suheli, the Maneating Tigress'. Here I shall only add that one day, hearing her admonishing the cub beyond a bend in the river, I sent my tracker to have a look. He hastened back to say that he was greeted by loud snarls. I rushed to the spot where Tara sat scowling in front of some heavy undergrowth which sheltered the cub. As I called to her her expression softened in recognition. The clock turned back for me as the span of years seemed to fade, and the past merged with the present.

Tara's other daughter opted for freedom, and Tara was ready to breed once more. Her Male appeared on cue and on 3 March 1986, two years to the day after the appearance of her second family, there arrived her third consisting of a male and a female. I often watched them in the water during the hot weather, and they grew apace on top of the escarpment during the monsoon. Soon after the appearance of the cubs, there arrived a large female with a pair of cubs from six to eight months old, apparently from another portion of Tara's Male's realm, for by the way that the male associated with them over a maggoty kill it appeared that they were his cubs. However, spacing calls from Tara induced the bigger tigress to abandon the range into which she had strayed to the suckling and less mobile female, and I watched Tara take a piece of intestine into the ravine where her latest cubs were hidden.

Shortly afterwards, as I walked along the north bank of the river, I heard low snarls which erupted into full-throated roars as Tara threatened me from across the river. I called to her, but she continued her demonstrations, and too late I realized that I had come between her and her cubs. She made a short mock charge along a log spanning the river, and branched off to continue a low-key growling from behind cover. I moved away, and soon the cubs joined the mother walking along the same log from where she had threatened me. However, as if to show that there was no ill feeling, when I called Tara the next morning while she was in the act of disappearing into the jungle, she stopped, looked in the direction from which I was calling, and turned about to walk past in the opposite direction. But I waited in vain for the prusten which would have sealed the bond of recognition. Perhaps my failing senses had let me down as they had the time before.

During the monsoon Tara's Male disappeared, and the Male Cub was last seen in August. But in September 1985 a stranger tiger appeared on the range with a diagnostically splayed toe on either forepaw, and I have described episodes connected with him in 'Splay Toes—Almost a Maneater'. I concluded that he was one of Tara's earlier cubs. For four months Splay Toes coexisted peaceably with Tara and her latest cubs. A certain order of precedence prevailed in their association, and though the younger tigers would give way when the elder male arrived, Splay Toes would also wait in the wings while the others fed, especially when he had not been the killer.

There was a kill by Tara on the night of 25–26 October 1988, and a loud calling in the morning. Later, at mid-day, a tiger crossed the metalled Palia-Dudhwa Road, and entered the Mating Copse adjoining Juliette Point, and there was a loud greeting roar late in the evening. The tiger was a large one with a rear pad overlap of about eight inches. On the morning of the 27th infrequent roars changed to moaning thrusts, and these, punctuated by the riposte of occasional roars by Tara, continued through the day and night. He came into the water, but was summoned by Tara to continue the mating ritual. Interestingly enough, it was Tara's Male who summoned the female previously when they mated for the first time, for perhaps the urgency varies as time elapses. In any case, they parted with a harsh roar on the morning of the 29th. However, four months later Tara came to a kill, and left droplets of milk on some grass, which filled me with elation: she had mothered her fourth family.

Before the rains, when the sun is at its hottest and driest, I walked a jungle path along the river. From up-stream Tara moaned, soft and low. As I approached, the magic sounds swelled as she called to her cubs. Suddenly, round a bend her head appeared, framed in a festoon of grass. For fifteen years we had trod the range, sometimes by day and occasionally by night; and now the time approached for Tara to vanish, perhaps to a Tiger Heaven, as her progenitors take over, for a while.

During February 1991 two young tigers courted and mated within the hearing of Tiger Haven, and their pugmarks were seen on the dirt track approaches. I then knew that the old order had changed. I wondered in what deep ravine Tara's bones reposed, for in the natural order death is known as evolution, and has no terrors of the hereafter.

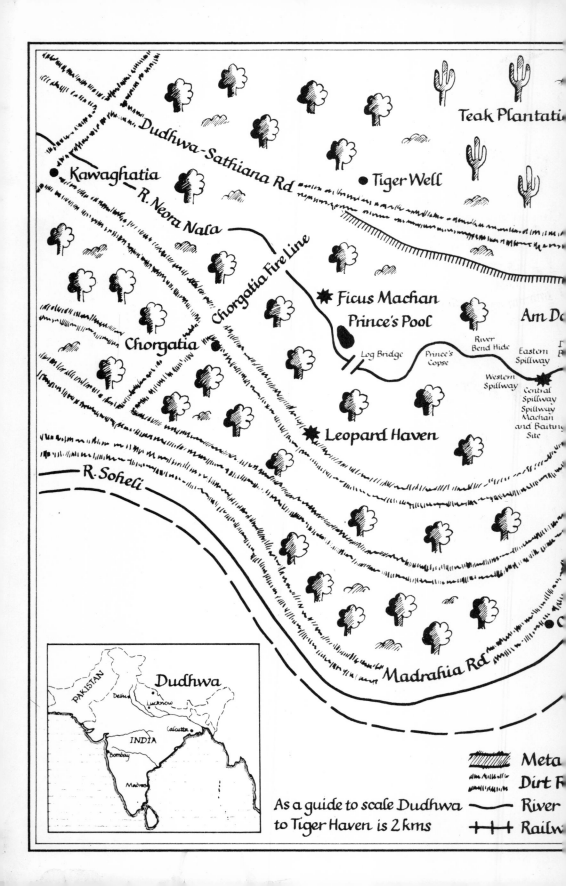

Dudhwa-Sathiana Rd

Kawaghatia

R. Neora Nala

Chorgatia Fire Line

Chorgatia

Tiger Well

Teak Plantati

Ficus Machan
Prince's Pool

Am D

Log Bridge

Prince's
Copse

River
Bend Hide

Eastern
Spillway

Western
Spillway

Central
Spillway
Spillway
Machan
and Baiting
Site

Leopard Haven

R. Soheli

Madrahia Rd

C

PAKISTAN

Dudhwa

Delhi

Lucknow

INDIA

Calcutta

Bombay

Madras

As a guide to scale Dudhwa
to Tiger Haven is 2 kms

Meta

Dirt R

River

Railw